DELAYED NOT DENIED

I0518867

Your Purpose Is Still Unfolding

By

Ethan L. Ketterer

DELAYED NOT DENIED

Printed in the United States of America

First Edition

ISBN: 979-8-9999942-2-6

DELAYED NOT DENIED

For bulk orders, speaking engagements, or ministry resources, contact: admin1@mykturn.com

DEDICATION

Dedicated to every believer who has ever waited, wondered, wrestled, and wept yet still held on to faith.

To the ones who prayed for doors that never opened, only to discover later that God was preparing a better path.
To those who endured long nights, silent seasons, and quiet battles that no one else saw but God did.
To the dreamers who kept showing up even when progress felt invisible.
To the warriors who refused to quit when delay tried to convince them that denial was their destiny.

This book is for you.

May these pages remind you that God has not forgotten you, His timing has not failed you, and His plans have not changed concerning you? Delayed does not mean denied your purpose is still unfolding.

And to everyone who encouraged me, prayed for me, and believed in the calling on my life, thank you. You helped me keep going when the wait felt long.

ACKNOWLEDGEMENTS

I Want to extend my deepest gratitude to everyone who has stood beside me on this journey. Writing Delayed Not Denied was not simply an act of putting words on pages it was a spiritual process, a personal reflection, and a testimony to God's faithfulness in every waiting season. I am grateful for every person who helped make this book possible.

To my wife thank you for your unwavering love, patience, and strength.
Your support has been a steady anchor in every season of delay, transition, and breakthrough. Thank you for believing in my calling, encouraging my dreams, and covering me in prayer. Your presence has been a gift from God, and I am forever grateful for you.

To my friends and loved ones who believed in my calling thank you for speaking life into me. Thank you for reminding me that the delays were only divine pauses, not permanent stops.

DELAYED NOT DENIED

To the readers, supporters, and the growing KTURN family thank you for embracing the message of hope, purpose, and perseverance. Your testimonies, messages, and encouragement continue to fuel the mission God placed in my heart. You are the reason I continue to write, inspire, and pour into projects that uplift and empower.

To every pastor, leader, mentor, and encourager who poured wisdom into my life your words have taken root. Your insight, prayers, and guidance have shaped the foundation upon which this book was built.

And above all, I give honor and glory to God.
The One who sustains, restores, redirects, and reveals.
The One who turns waiting into wisdom, delays into development, and closed doors into greater opportunities.
Without Him, this work would not exist.

Thank you to everyone who played a part visible or unseen. Your support is deeply appreciated, and your impact will always be remembered.

TABLE OF CONTENTS

DELAYED NOT DENIED...1

DEDICATION ii

ACKNOWLEDGEMENTS iii

CHAPTER 1 1

CHAPTER 2 12

CHAPTER 3 25

CHAPTER 4 35

CHAPTER 5 46

CHAPTER 6 59

CHAPTER 7 73

CHAPTER 8 87

CHAPTER 9 100

CHAPTER 10 112

CHAPTER 11 125

CHAPTER 12 137

CHAPTER 13 150

CHAPTER 14 163

CHAPTER 15 171

CHAPTER 16 176

CHAPTER 17 182

CHAPTER 18 186

CHAPTER 19 194

CHAPTER 20 199

FINAL PRAYER.. 204

REFLECTION 207

ABOUT THE AUTHOR... 220

CHAPTER 1

WHEN LIFE HITS PAUSE

Life rarely asks our permission before shifting direction. One moment everything feels aligned your strength is steady, your plans seem clear, and your momentum feels unstoppable. You're walking with expectation, believing that the next step will carry you closer to what God has promised. Then suddenly, and without warning, everything slows down. Movement becomes stillness. Clarity becomes confusion. What once felt certain now feels distant. In a single moment, **life hits pause.**

These pauses shake us because they disrupt our sense of timing and challenge our understanding of God's process. We often associate forward motion with favor, and stillness with something gone wrong. But Scripture reminds us that God is deeply involved even in our still moments.

"Be still, and know that I am God."
— *Psalm 46:10 (KJV)*

Stillness is not punishment it's revelation. It's where God reminds us that He is in control, even when life feels out of control.

Before we understand the purpose of the pause, we often feel the pain of it. But every divine pause carries meaning.

THE DAY EVERYTHING STOPPED

If you reflect on your life, you can likely identify a moment where everything shifted a conversation, a situation, a choice, or an interruption that placed your momentum on hold. For some, it was sudden. For others, subtle. But for everyone, it was impactful.

Pauses don't always come as storms. Sometimes they come quietly:

A delayed opportunity

A dream that takes longer than expected

A transition that disrupts your plans

A season where nothing seems to move

A door that closes unexpectedly

These moments carry weight because we feel them deeply. Yet even in these shifts, God's sovereignty remains unshaken.

"The steps of a good man are ordered by the LORD: and he delighteth in his way."
— *Psalm 37:23 (KJV)*

When life hits pause, your steps are not cancelled sthey are being *ordered*. God is not confused by the pause. He designed it.

WHY PAUSES FEEL SO PAINFUL

Pauses confront our desire for progress. We crave movement because movement feels like proof that we're on track. When movement stops, doubt rises:

- "Am I still in God's will?"
- "Did I miss my moment?"
- "Is God disappointed in me?"
- "Why did this stop now?"

These questions arise not because we lack faith, but because we are human. Even David wrestled with delay and divine silence.

"How long wilt thou forget me, O LORD? Forever? how long wilt thou hide thy face from me?"
— *Psalm 13:1 (KJV)*

But despite David's questions, God's promise to him never changed.

And neither has God's promise to you.

Pauses feel painful because they challenge our timelines, but God is not governed by time. He governs *purpose*.

THE QUESTIONS WE DON'T SAY OUT LOUD

In seasons of pausing, our inner dialogue becomes louder. We wrestle with doubts we would never voice in public. But Scripture gives us permission to bring our concerns before God.

"Cast thy burden upon the LORD, and he shall sustain thee."
— *Psalm 55:22 (KJV)*

God does not silence you in your questioning—He sustains you in it.

Behind every pause is a question. Behind every question is a desire for understanding. And behind every desire for understanding is a deeper longing to trust God fully.

WHEN GOD INTERRUPTS YOUR PLANS

Interruptions are often divine interventions disguised as inconvenience. God pauses us not to punish us but to redirect us. He slows us down when continuing forward would cause more harm than good.

Some of the doors God closed were never meant to open. Some of the opportunities that slipped away were not tied to your destiny. Some of the people who left could not walk with you into the next season.

"For my thoughts are not your thoughts, neither are your ways my ways, saith the LORD."
— *Isaiah 55:8 (KJV)*

His ways are higher. His timing is greater. His pauses are purposeful.

Many things you cried over losing were actually God removing what was blocking your growth.

PAUSE IS NOT FAILURE

Our culture glorifies speed, but the Kingdom of God values **process**.

"The vision is yet for an appointed time… though it tarry, wait for it; because it will surely come, it will not tarry."
— *Habakkuk 2:3 (KJV)*

God has *appointed times* for everything He has promised. Delays do not erase those appointments—they prepare you for them.

You cannot miss what God has ordained.

You cannot be late to what God has scheduled.

You cannot be denied from what God designed for you.

The pause is not failure—it is formation.

PAUSES EXPOSE THE HEART

Stillness reveals truth. When life slows down, we meet parts of ourselves that were hidden behind busyness:

- Old wounds
- Fears
- Doubts
- Unhealed places
- Misguided expectations

But exposure is not meant to embarrass you—it's meant to *heal* you.

"Search me, O God, and know my heart: try me, and know my thoughts."
— *Psalm 139:23 (KJV)*

Pauses help us see what God already sees. They are invitations to deeper transformation.

THE PAUSE THAT BUILDS YOU

While you wait, God works. His work may be invisible, but it is intentional.

1. Spiritual Strengthening

"But they that wait upon the LORD shall renew their strength."
— *Isaiah 40:31 (KJV)*

Waiting renews what rushing would have depleted.

2. Emotional Maturity

Delay teaches us to respond instead of react, to trust instead of panic.

3. Patience and Endurance

"Knowing this, that the trying of your faith worketh patience."
— *James 1:3 (KJV)*

Without trials, patience would remain undeveloped.

4. Clarity and Discernment

Stillness sharpens your spiritual hearing.

5. Wisdom for Future Seasons

Lessons learned in waiting become tools used in destiny.

Nothing learned in the pause is wasted.

BIBLICAL PAUSES WITH PURPOSE

Every major biblical figure experienced God-ordained delays:

Joseph

His delay in prison became his pathway to the palace.

"But the LORD was with Joseph…"
— *Genesis 39:21 (KJV)*

Moses

His 40-year pause prepared him to lead millions out of bondage.

Hannah

Her delay birthed Samuel, a prophet whose influence shaped Israel.

David

His years in hiding strengthened him for the throne.

"Wait on the LORD: be of good courage…"
— *Psalm 27:14 (KJV)*

Paul

His pauses shaped his mission and birthed much of the New Testament.

God specializes in turning waiting places into birthing places.

WHEN YOU FEEL BEHIND

One of the enemy's greatest lies is that you are running out of time. That others are ahead of you. That you've missed your moment. But Scripture refutes that lie entirely.

"There is a time there for every purpose and for every work." — *Ecclesiastes 3:17 (KJV)*

Purpose has its own timetable—set by God, not by comparison.

You are not late—you are aligned.

THE TURNING POINT

Every pause eventually leads to a divine turning point. You will one day look back and say:

- "God was protecting me."
- "God was preparing me."
- "God was strengthening me."
- "God was redirecting me."

- "God was preserving me for something greater."

The pause will make sense in hindsight. It always does.

YOU ARE STILL MOVING, EVEN HERE

The absence of visible progress does not mean the absence of spiritual progress.

God is working behind the scenes:

- Aligning relationships
- Preparing opportunities
- Clearing obstacles
- Strengthening your character
- Healing unseen wounds
- Orchestrating divine timing

"For we walk by faith, not by sight."
— *2 Corinthians 5:7 (KJV)*

You may not see movement, but heaven is moving on your behalf.

REFLECTION QUESTIONS — CHAPTER 1

1. What moment in your life best represents "the day everything stopped"?

2. How have you typically interpreted pauses—punishment or protection?

3. What scripture from this chapter speaks most to your current season?

4. What hidden thoughts or emotions has this pause revealed?

5. What might God be preparing or protecting you from in this season?

6. How have past delays shaped your faith or strengthened you?

JOURNALING PROMPT — CHAPTER 1

"Lord, if this pause is part of your preparation, show me what you are developing in me."

Write freely. Let the Holy Spirit lead your pen.

CHAPTER 2

THE WEIGHT OF WAITING

THE WEIGHT OF WAITING

Waiting is one of the heaviest experiences a believer can endure. It presses against the heart, stretches the mind, and tests the spirit in ways that defy simple explanation. The weight of waiting is not just the passage of time — it is the emotional, spiritual, and psychological toll that comes with hoping for something you cannot yet touch. It is believing for something you cannot yet see. It is trusting God when circumstances tell you no, when timelines tell you you're late, and when feelings tell you to quit.

Waiting is both a burden and a blessing.
A hardship and a holy place.
A test and a teacher.

And every believer — no matter how strong — must carry the weight of waiting at some point in their journey.

THE INVISIBLE BURDEN THAT NO ONE RECOGNIZES

There is a weight you carry in your waiting that others rarely see. People may notice you showing up, smiling, pressing through your day-to-day responsibilities, but they don't always see the silent battles:

- The prayers you whisper before bed
- The sighs you release when no one is looking
- The moments of questioning that rise in your spirit
- The emotional fatigue that sits beneath your smile
- The faith you fight to maintain
- The patience you struggle to keep

You can function and still feel fatigued.

You can work and still feel weary.

You can keep moving and still feel stuck.

Scripture acknowledges this inner heaviness clearly:

"My soul melteth for heaviness: strengthen thou me according unto thy word."
— *Psalm 119:28 (KJV)*

This verse captures the truth: waiting doesn't always weaken the body — it weakens the soul.

But God offers strength *according to His Word* — not according to your feelings, your timeline, or your understanding.

Your heart may feel overwhelmed, but Heaven remains in complete control.

THE DELAY THAT DRAINS YOU

The hardest part of waiting is the *uncertainty*. If God told you that your breakthrough would arrive in exactly six months, your faith would grow, your patience would settle, and your emotions would stabilize. But God rarely reveals timelines.

He reveals Himself.
He reveals His promises.
He reveals His faithfulness.

But He rarely reveals *when* the promise will manifest.

That is where the draining begins.

Waiting drains you because:

- You don't know how long the delay will last
- You can't predict what will happen next
- You can't see the progress God is making behind the scenes
- You wonder if something has gone wrong

- You feel pressure to remain strong for others
- You battle doubt, fear, and discouragement
- You question if anything is changing at all

And in that emotional tension, the enemy whispers lies:

- "God forgot you."
- "You missed your moment."
- "You prayed in vain."
- "Everyone else is moving but you."
- "Your promise is slipping away."

But the Word exposes every lie the enemy speaks:

"And let us not be weary in well doing: for in due season we shall reap, if we faint not."
— *Galatians 6:9 (KJV)*

Your due season is real.

Your reaping is guaranteed.

Your responsibility is simply: **don't faint.**

The enemy can delay your emotions, but he cannot deny your destiny.

THE PRUNING OF PATIENCE

Waiting is not only emotional — it is spiritual surgery. God uses seasons of delay to prune us, refine us, and shape us into people who can carry the weight of His blessings.

Jesus explained the pruning process clearly:

"Every branch that beareth fruit, he purgeth it, that it may bring forth more fruit."
— *John 15:2 (KJV)*

To "purge" or prune is to:

- Cut away what drains you
- Remove what hinders you
- Reduce what slows you
- Strengthen what remains
- Prepare you for increase

Waiting trims away:

- Impatience
- Impulsiveness
- Immature expectations
- Emotional instability
- Panic-based decision-making
- Relationships that are seasonal, not lifelong

- Priorities that do not align with purpose

God is not *subtracting* from you — He is *strategically shaping* you.

The weight you feel is not just from waiting — it's from being pruned into your future.

LONELINESS IN THE WAITING ROOM

One of the most difficult parts of waiting is the loneliness that settles in your heart. You may stand in crowds yet feel unseen. You may hear others testify about blessings while you quietly ask, "Lord, when will it happen for me?" You may support others with genuine joy, yet go home with silent tears.

Waiting can feel lonely.
Waiting can feel isolating.
Waiting can feel like Heaven is quiet and people are distant.

But Scripture speaks directly to that feeling:

"I will never leave thee, nor forsake thee."
— *Hebrews 13:5 (KJV)*

God stays in the waiting room with you.
He sits beside you in the silence.

He strengthens you in the sorrow.

He comforts you in the loneliness.

People may not understand the weight you carry — but God carries it with you.

WAITING IS WORKING — EVEN WHEN NOTHING SEEMS TO BE CHANGING

Waiting feels passive, but spiritually, waiting is one of the most *active* things you will ever do.

Waiting builds qualities that speed could never produce:

1. Trust without Evidence

"Trust in the LORD with all thine heart; and lean not unto thine own understanding."
— *Proverbs 3:5 (KJV)*

Trust that is built without answers is trust that cannot be shaken.

2. Internal Strength

David experienced this:

"But David encouraged himself in the LORD his God."
— *1 Samuel 30:6 (KJV)*

Waiting seasons teach you how to speak life over yourself when no one else knows what you're carrying.

3. Faith That Survives Silence

"For we walk by faith, not by sight."
— *2 Corinthians 5:7 (KJV)*

Sight needs proof.
Faith only needs God.

4. Patience That Matures Character

"The trying of your faith worketh patience."
— *James 1:3 (KJV)*

Patience is not learned in blessing — it is learned in delay.

5. Surrender and Release

Waiting reminds you that you are not in control — God is.

Your waiting is working, even when your eyes see nothing happening.

THE DANGER OF RUSHING AHEAD OF GOD

The longer you wait, the stronger the temptation to rush becomes.

Waiting whispers:

"Maybe I should help God."

"Maybe I should speed this up."

"Maybe I should force something to happen."

But anything you force outside of God's timing becomes a burden inside of God's promise.

Abraham discovered this truth when impatience birthed Ishmael.

The promise still came through Isaac — but the consequences of moving ahead of God lingered for generations.

There is always a cost to rushed decisions.

There is always peace attached to God's timing.

Your Isaac — your true promise — is worth waiting for.

THE WISDOM GAINED ONLY THROUGH WAITING

Waiting seasons are often the most transformative seasons of your life. They teach you lessons you could not learn in comfort or speed.

Waiting produces:

- **Discernment** — the ability to identify what is God and what is not
- **Spiritual depth** — stronger prayer life and closer dependence on God
- **Emotional maturity** — responding instead of reacting
- **Wisdom** — understanding that timing is as important as blessing
- **Boundaries** — identifying who belongs in this season
- **Humility** — knowing that God holds the pen, not you

Wisdom is the reward of waiting well.

THE WEIGHTS THAT SHAPED DESTINY

Every major destiny in Scripture involved waiting:

Joseph waited in pits and prisons

His character was strengthened before he ever touched the palace.

Hannah waited with sorrow

Her worship was deepened before God opened her womb.

DELAYED NOT DENIED

Moses waited 40 years in the desert

His humility replaced impulsiveness.

David waited between anointing and appointing

His heart was tested before his throne was established.

Jesus Himself waited 30 years

Before stepping into a ministry that changed the world.

Delay is not a sign of denial — it is the soil of destiny.

THE RENEWAL PROMISE

God gives a unique promise to those who wait:

"They that wait upon the LORD shall renew their
strength…"
— *Isaiah 40:31 (KJV)*

Not might
Not may
Not possibly

"Shall."

Waiting does not drain you — it renews you.
Waiting does not weaken you — it strengthens you.
Waiting does not waste time — it redeems time.

Every moment you think you're losing is actually being invested into your future.

REFLECTION QUESTIONS — CHAPTER 2

1. What emotions rise within you during long waiting seasons?
2. How has waiting challenged your relationship with God?
3. What burdens in this season feel invisible to those around you?
4. Where do you see pruning happening in your life?
5. What rushed decisions have you avoided because you chose to wait on God?
6. What new wisdom is God forming in you?
7. Which Scripture in this chapter brings the most peace to your heart?

JOURNALING PROMPT — CHAPTER 2

"Father, show me what you are cultivating in me through this season of waiting. Reveal what You are strengthening, pruning, or preparing in my life."

DELAYED NOT DENIED

Write freely. Let the Spirit minister and speak.

CHAPTER 3

QUESTIONS WITHOUT ANSWERS

There are few things more difficult for the human heart than carrying questions God has not yet answered. When circumstances shift unexpectedly, when delays stretch longer than anticipated, or when prayers remain unfulfilled, the soul begins to whisper inquiries that feel too heavy to speak aloud. These questions don't always come from disbelief — they often come from disappointment, confusion, or wounded hope.

Every believer has stood in a season where questions multiplied while answers remained silent.

And though these questions may feel unsettling, Scripture shows us that God allows space for them. He does not silence our searching. He does not shame our wondering. He does not punish our wrestling. Instead, He invites us to bring our questions to Him.

"Call unto me, and I will answer thee, and show thee great and mighty things, which thou knowest not."
— *Jeremiah 33:3 (KJV)*

God does not forbid questions — He invites them.

He only asks that we bring them to Him, not away from Him.

WHEN LIFE DOESN'T MAKE SENSE

When you're facing a delay, when breakthrough hasn't come, when prayers seem unanswered, you may ask:

- "Lord, why hasn't this changed yet?"
- "When will I see the fulfillment of your promise?"
- "Why did you allow this setback?"
- "Why them, Lord, and not me?"
- "What am I supposed to learn from this?"
- "How long must I carry this burden?"
- "Is there something wrong with me?"

These are the questions that echo in the silence.

These are the questions that keep us awake at night.

These are the questions that test the soul.

Even David, a man after God's own heart, wrestled with unanswered questions:

"How long wilt thou forget me, O LORD? forever? how long wilt thou hide thy face from me?"

— *Psalm 13:1 (KJV)*

David didn't hide his frustration — he brought it to God.

His honesty did not disqualify him — it drew God closer.

THE DISCOMFORT OF DIVINE SILENCE

One of the hardest parts of faith is enduring God's silence.

Not His absence — just His silence. Because silence can feel like distance, even though God is right beside you.

Silence in Scripture is often a sign of:

- God listening
- God preparing
- God protecting
- God positioning
- God testing
- God strengthening
- God developing faith
- God accomplishing something unseen

Silence is not divine punishment.

Silence is divine strategy.

When Heaven is quiet, God is working.

"Behold, the LORD's hand is not shortened, that it cannot save; neither his ear heavy, that it cannot hear."

— *Isaiah 59:1 (KJV)*

Your prayers did not bounce off the ceiling.

God heard the first time — He is simply working in ways you cannot yet see.

QUESTIONS THAT REVEAL THE HEART

Some questions aren't about information — they're about revelation.

They reveal:

- Where your trust is anchored
- Where your hope is fragile
- Where your wounds still linger
- Where your expectations need clarity
- Where your understanding needs surrender
- Where your faith is being refined

Questions are not the enemy of faith — unanswered questions *shape* faith.

You do not grow by knowing everything.

You grow by trusting God when you know almost nothing.

WHEN ANSWERS DELAY BUT GOD REMAINS FAITHFUL

Sometimes God does not answer the question we ask — but He answers the part of us that needed healing. You may be asking for clarity, but God responds with comfort. You may be asking for a timeline, but God responds with peace. You may be asking "when," but God answers "trust Me."

"In all thy ways acknowledge him, and he shall direct thy paths."
— *Proverbs 3:6 (KJV)*

God directs paths before He explains them.
He leads before He defines the destination.

When answers delay, guidance still flows.

WHEN QUESTIONS TURN TO DOUBT

Unanswered questions can open the door to doubt if not surrendered to God.

You may find yourself wondering:

- "Is God still working?"
- "Did I misunderstand His promise?"
- "Is the delay my fault?"
- "Has God changed His mind about me?"

But Scripture anchors the heart:

"For the gifts and calling of God are without repentance."
— *Romans 11:29 (KJV)*

God does not change His mind about you.

God does not retract His promise.

God does not cancel your calling.

Delay cannot remove what God has ordained.

THE TRANSFORMATION HIDDEN IN QUESTIONS

There is a transformation happening inside you as you wrestle with questions you cannot answer. God uses the tension to deepen:

- Your dependency on Him
- Your sensitivity to His voice
- Your awareness of His sovereignty
- Your understanding of His heart
- Your resilience in adversity
- Your maturity in spiritual discipline

Questions stretch you.

Silence strengthens you.

Waiting stabilizes you.

Faith sustains you.

What you're becoming in the process is just as important as what you're waiting for.

WHAT TO DO WHEN GOD DOESN'T EXPLAIN

When answers do not come, Scripture offers direction:

1. Keep trusting God
"Commit thy way unto the LORD; trust also in him; and he shall bring it to pass."
— *Psalm 37:5 (KJV)*

Trust is obedience in uncertainty.

2. Keep praying
"Men ought always to pray, and not to faint."
— *Luke 18:1 (KJV)*

Prayer is spiritual oxygen.98'

3. Keep believing the promise
"For all the promises of God in him are yea, and in him Amen."
— *2 Corinthians 1:20 (KJV)*

Promises outlast problems.

4. Keep walking by faith
"For we walk by faith, not by sight."
— *2 Corinthians 5:7 (KJV)*

Your next step does not require full explanation.

5. Keep worshiping
Worship clears the fog that questions create.

"I will bless the LORD at all times."
— *Psalm 34:1 (KJV)*

Worship invites clarity even without answers.

THE PEACE GOD GIVES WHEN ANSWERS DON'T

There is a unique peace that God gives not *after* answers appear, but *before*.

"And the peace of God, which passeth all understanding, shall keep your hearts and minds through Christ Jesus."
— *Philippians 4:7 (KJV)*

This peace protects you while you wait for understanding.
It guards your mind while delay stretches.
It stabilizes your emotions while silence lingers.

Peace is God's answer while you wait for answers.

WHEN THE ANSWER IS "WAIT"

Sometimes the answer is not "yes" or "no."
Sometimes it is **"wait — I am working."**

DELAYED NOT DENIED

If God has not spoken yet, it's because:

- The blessing isn't ready
- *You're* not fully ready
- The environment isn't ready
- The people connected to your promise aren't ready
- The timing isn't aligned
- The testimony isn't complete

Waiting is not denial — it's divine arrangement.

God is standing behind the scenes orchestrating what you prayed for.

YOUR QUESTIONS WILL ONE DAY BECOME TESTIMONY

There will come a moment when the very question you're asking today will become the testimony you share tomorrow.

You will look back and say:

- "Now I understand why He delayed."
- "Now I see what He was protecting me from."
- "Now I realize He was preparing me."
- "Now I know that the wait was worth it."

Your confusion will one day turn to clarity.

Your waiting will one day turn to worship.

Your questions will one day turn to revelation.

REFLECTION QUESTIONS — CHAPTER 3

1. What unanswered questions weigh most heavily on your heart right now?
2. How do you typically respond when God is silent?
3. Which Scripture in this chapter brought you the most comfort?
4. Where do you sense God asking you to trust Him without full explanation?
5. How might God be using unanswered questions to strengthen your faith?
6. What promise do you need to hold onto despite uncertainty?

JOURNALING PROMPT — CHAPTER 3

"Lord, teach me to trust you even when I do not understand your timing or your plan. Reveal the peace that comes from surrendering unanswered questions into Your hands."

Write freely. Let honesty and faith meet on the page.

CHAPTER 4

WHEN DOORS CLOSE WITHOUT WARNING

Doors represent possibility. They represent movement, transition, momentum, and direction. A door opening feels like favor. A door staying open feels like stability. But when a door closes—especially one you prayed for, prepared for, or believed for—it can feel like confusion and loss.

Closed doors confront us. They challenge our expectations and push us into a deeper level of trust. They force us to acknowledge something we often overlook:

God's sovereignty is not only seen in open doors — it is also seen in the ones He shuts.

"He openeth, and no man shutteth; and shutteth, and no man openeth."
— *Revelation 3:7 (KJV)*

If God shuts it, nothing can reopen it.
If God blocks it, nothing can bypass His will.
If God interrupts it, He is intervening for your good.

God's closures are acts of compassion, not cruelty.

THE DOORS WE EXPECT TO STAY OPEN

We often build our expectations around the doors we believe will remain open:

- The job we thought we'd retire from
- The relationship we thought was forever
- The ministry role we thought was permanent
- The opportunity we thought was guaranteed
- The door that had momentum but suddenly froze
- The plan we laid out in detail but God suddenly halted

It's disorienting when something we trusted unexpectedly changes.

The human heart prefers predictability. We want a sense of control. But faith operates in a realm where only God knows what lies behind every door.

"A man's heart deviseth his way: but the LORD directeth his steps."
— *Proverbs 16:9 (KJV)*

You may plan your path — but God controls every doorway.

THE SHOCK OF SUDDEN CLOSURE

There are closures you see coming — you sense the shift, feel the drift, and recognize the signs. But the most difficult closures are the ones you *never saw coming*.

When the unexpected happens:

- A contract falls through
- A ministry season ends abruptly

- A relationship shifts overnight
- A promotion is given to someone else
- A partnership dissolves
- A service, opportunity, or open door shuts instantly

Sudden closures hit differently. They shake your footing. They challenge your emotional equilibrium. They make you question what you thought you heard God say.

But sudden closures are often the clearest signs of God's direct involvement.

Sometimes God closes a door gently.
Other times He shuts it loudly so you won't try to reopen it.

Sudden stops are often divine rescues in disguise.

THE DOOR THAT SHOULD HAVE OPENED… BUT DIDN'T

There are times when you did everything right — you prayed, prepared, worked, believed — and the door still closed.

That kind of closure is painful.
That kind of closure feels personal.
That kind of closure interrupts the heart.

You may ask:

- "Lord, didn't you lead me here?"
- "Wasn't this opportunity from you?"
- "Why would you allow me to get this close?"

But Scripture teaches that God guides in layers:

"Thy word is a lamp unto my feet, and a light unto my path."
— *Psalm 119:105 (KJV)*

A lamp shows just enough to take the next step — not the entire journey.

Sometimes God lets you walk toward a door because the *journey* is the lesson, not the entry.

You were supposed to walk *to it*,
but not *through it*.

WHEN A CLOSED DOOR SAVES YOUR FUTURE

You do not always know what is behind a door — but God does.
You do not always foresee what a door will require — but God does.
You cannot see hidden traps, unseen dangers, wrong connections, or spiritual attacks — but God does.

A closed door is not just protection from the past — it is protection for the *future*.

Think of Joseph:

- His brothers closed the door of family.
- Potiphar's wife closed the door of reputation.
- The cupbearer closed the door of remembrance.

Yet every closure moved Joseph closer to purpose — not further away.

"But God meant it unto good…"
— *Genesis 50:20 (KJV)*

Closed doors are strategic, not accidental.

WHEN GOD CLOSES A DOOR BECAUSE YOU OUTGREW IT

Not every closure is about danger — some closures happen because you have **outgrown** what's behind the door.

There are seasons where:

- Your anointing outgrows your environment
- Your calling outgrows your circle
- Your character outgrows old habits
- Your purpose outgrows old relationships
- Your vision outgrows people who cannot support it
- Your faith outgrows fear-based decisions

Sometimes God closes a door not because what's behind it is evil — but because it is *too small* for where He is taking you.

"Enlarge the place of thy tent…"
— *Isaiah 54:2 (KJV)*

You cannot expand while clinging to what is shrinking.

THE SEASON OF DIVINE BLOCKING

You may not realize it, but **God blocks things every day**:

- Opportunities that would have drained you
- Relationships that would have broken you
- Jobs that would have limited you
- Invitations that were not aligned with destiny
- Plans that were too small
- Paths that were too dangerous
- People who were not assigned to your future

Blocking is a form of blessing.

Blockage is not denial — it is divine direction.

God loves you too much to let you walk through certain doors.

WHEN A CLOSED DOOR BREAKS YOUR HEART

Let's be honest: not all closures feel holy.

Some closures break something inside you.
Some closures bruise your expectations.
Some closures wounded your trust.
Some closures made you question your discernment.
Some closures made you afraid to try again.

When your heart breaks at a closed door, remember this promise:

"The LORD is nigh unto them that are of a broken heart..."
— *Psalm 34:18 (KJV)*

God draws closer in closed-door seasons.

He does not stand on the other side of the door — He stands beside you in the hallway.

THE HALLWAY BETWEEN DOORS

When a door closes, there is often a hallway season — an in-between space where you feel suspended between where you were and where you're going.

The hallway season can feel:

- Confusing
- Quiet
- Unsettling
- Overwhelming
- Uncertain

- Directionless

But hallways serve a holy purpose.

Hallways are where:

- God recalibrates your spirit
- God detoxes your heart
- God prepares the new assignment
- God strengthens your identity
- God restores your confidence
- God realigns your focus

Hallways are not permanent.
Hallways are transitional.

And God meets His children in the hallway.

WHEN CLOSURES FEEL LIKE SETBACKS

Closed doors often feel like steps backwards, but in the Kingdom, a setback is usually a **setup**.

God never shuts a door without preparing a better one:

"For a great door and effectual is opened unto me…"
— *1 Corinthians 16:9 (KJV)*

Great doors often come after closed ones.

Closed doors:

- Reposition you
- Redirect you
- Realign you
- Refocus you
- Reinforce your dependence on God

God cannot elevate you while you are clinging to something beneath your level.

THE DOOR THAT WILL OPEN NEXT

God already knows which door He will open next for you. It is not random. It is not accidental. It is intentional, strategic, and tailor-made for your calling.

The next door will be:

- Bigger
- Better
- Stronger
- Clearer
- More aligned
- More fruitful
- More secure
- More anointed
- More purposeful

And when it opens, you will realize:

The closed door was the best thing that could have happened.

HOW TO RESPOND WHEN GOD CLOSES A DOOR

1. Don't force it.

If God shut it, let it stay shut.

2. Don't internalize it.

Closed doors are not reflections of your worth.

3. Don't panic.

This is not the end of the story.

4. Don't complain.
Gratitude clears your vision.

5. Don't stop walking with God.
The next step is coming.

6. Don't reopen what God closed.
Reopening a God-closed door invites unnecessary trouble.

7. Don't lose hope.
Closed doors lead to divine redirection.

8. Don't disconnect from prayer.
Prayer is your navigation system in hallway seasons.

WHAT CLOSED DOORS TEACH YOU

Closed doors teach:

- Discernment
- Patience
- Humility
- Faith
- Boundary setting
- Emotional maturity
- Trust beyond understanding
- Sensitivity to God's voice
- How to let go
- How to pivot
- How to surrender your will

Closed doors do not decrease you — they **develop** you.

THE GIFT OF A CLOSED DOOR

Some blessings will only make sense later:

- Years later, you will thank God for who He removed.
- Years later, you will thank God for what didn't work out.
- Years later, you will thank God for the prayers He didn't answer.
- Years later, you will thank God for interrupting your plans.

Closed doors become praise reports in hindsight.

REFLECTION QUESTIONS — CHAPTER 4

1. What door closed recently that you still do not understand?
2. How did that closure affect your faith, confidence, or emotions?
3. Do you tend to interpret closures as rejection or protection?
4. Which Scripture in this chapter speaks to your situation most strongly?
5. What do you sense God may be protecting or redirecting you from?
6. What part of your life feels like a hallway right now?
7. What new door do you feel God preparing you for?

JOURNALING PROMPT — CHAPTER 4

"Father, help me to see your hand in the doors you have closed. Reveal what You are preparing, protecting, and positioning in my life. Give me peace as I wait for the next door You will open."

Write openly and honestly. Let the Holy Spirit guide your reflection.

DELAYED NOT DENIED

CHAPTER 5

WRESTLING WITH GOD'S TIMING

Timing is one of the greatest mysteries of God. You can understand His promises, trust His character, believe His Word, and still wrestle with *when* those promises will come to pass. You may know **what** God said. You may even see **how** He's preparing you. But the **when** often remains hidden behind the veil of divine sovereignty.

This gap between promise and fulfillment is the place where faith is both tested and strengthened.

Every believer eventually enters a season where timing becomes a battle — a silent wrestling match between what you feel, what you hope for, and what God has not yet revealed.

THE TENSION BETWEEN NOW AND NOT YET

There is a unique tension that lives inside the heart of every waiting believer. It is the tension between:

- "I believe God…"

  and

- "But I don't understand His timing."

You can trust God completely and still wrestle with the pace of His plan.

You can walk in faith and still ache for clarity.
You can obey God and still wonder why things are taking so long.
You can be grateful for what you have and still long for what God promised.

This tension is not faithlessness — it is humanity.

Even the strongest believers struggled with timing:

"My times are in thy hand…"
— *Psalm 31:15 (KJV)*

David didn't say "my blessings" or "my breakthroughs" or "my opportunities."
He said **my times** — the schedule, the pacing, the timeline of his life — are in God's hands.

God owns the clock.
God controls the calendar.
God manages the seasons.

But knowing that doesn't always remove the wrestling.

WHEN GOD'S TIMING FEELS TOO SLOW

There are moments when you're certain the blessing is near, when everything seems aligned, and when you believe, "Surely, this is the moment."

But then — nothing happens.

Silence returns.

The pace slows again.

The door remains closed.

The answer is delayed.

The breakthrough is postponed.

And frustration rises.

You may find yourself praying:

- "Lord, why is this taking so long?"
- "Why haven't you moved yet?"
- "What am I missing?"
- "Is something wrong with me?"
- "Did I hear you correctly?"
- "How much longer must I wait?"

You're not alone. Scripture captures this beautifully:

"How long, O LORD?"

— *Psalm 13:1 (KJV)*

If David — a worshiper, warrior, king, and man after God's own heart — cried out "How long?", then your wrestling is not a lack of faith.

It's a sign you're stretching into spiritual maturity.

GOD'S TIMING VS. YOUR EXPECTATION

The hardest part of trusting God is releasing your expectations of when things *should* happen.

You may expect:

- The promotion this year
- The breakthrough this month
- The opportunity this season
- The relationship by now
- The healing at this stage
- The clarity by this point in the journey

But God's timing often differs from your expectation.

Sometimes radically.

You may want it **now**, but God wants you **ready**.

You may want it **quick**, but God wants it **complete**.

You may want it **soon**, but God wants it **strong**.

You may want it **now**, but God is aligning things for **later**.

He sees the full picture — you only see the moment.

"For my thoughts are not your thoughts, neither are your ways my ways, saith the LORD."
— *Isaiah 55:8 (KJV)*

Your timing is based on desire.
God's timing is based on destiny.

WHEN GOD'S TIMING FEELS TOO LATE

There are moments when the delay feels so long that you worry:

- "Has my season passed?"
- "Did I miss my opportunity?"
- "Is it too late for what I'm believing for?"
- "Has the window closed?"
- "Has God moved on without me?"

But Scripture speaks directly to these fears.

"To everything there is a season, and a time to every purpose under the heaven."
— *Ecclesiastes 3:1 (KJV)*

If there is **a time** for every purpose, then your purpose **has a time**.

And God alone determines when that time arrives.

When Lazarus died, Martha said:

"Lord, if thou hadst been here…"
— *John 11:21 (KJV)*

Her statement reveals what many of us think:

"Lord, You're late."

But Jesus responded:

"Said I not unto thee, that, if thou wouldest believe, thou shouldest see the glory of God?"
— *John 11:40 (KJV)*

God was not late — He was preparing a greater testimony.

THE PURPOSE OF DELAYED TIMING

God delays timing for reasons that often do not make sense until much later. His delays are intentional and strategic.

1. to strengthen your faith
Faith must be stretched to grow.

2. to prepare your character
Blessings require maturity to sustain them.

3. to align external conditions
God waits until the environment is ready.

4. to remove the wrong people
Some blessings can only flourish when certain people are no longer in your circle.

5. to position you correctly
Timing is part of placement — not just scheduling.

6. to protect you from premature success
An unprepared blessing can become a burden.

7. to build perseverance
You cannot carry greatness with shallow endurance.

8. to reveal your dependence on Him
Waiting purifies your motives.

God's delays always have purpose — even when you do not see it yet.

THE STRUGGLE BETWEEN PATIENCE AND PRESSURE

While waiting, you often face two competing voices:

The voice of patience:

"God is in control."

The voice of pressure:

"Do something before it's too late."

Pressure pushes you to force, compromise, or settle.

Patience invites you to trust, surrender, and wait.

The battle is real.

Paul understood this wrestling:

"For we are saved by hope: but hope that is seen is not hope…"
— *Romans 8:24 (KJV)*

Hope thrives where answers are absent.

BIBLICAL EXAMPLES OF DIVINE TIMING

ABRAHAM & SARAH — the Wait That Built a Nation
God promised a child.

Years passed.

Doubt grew.

Impatience birthed Ishmael.

But God's promise remained.

Isaac came *on time* — not early, not late.

JOSEPH — the Dreamer Delayed

Joseph waited 13 years — between pit, slavery, betrayal, false accusation, and prison.

But when his moment came, timing accelerated.

"Then Pharaoh sent and called Joseph…"
— *Genesis 41:14 (KJV)*

One call changed everything.

DAVID — Anointed but Not Appointed

Anointed as king in youth.

Appointed as king in adulthood.

The waiting built his heart.

JESUS — God's Timing in Human Form

Jesus lived 30 years before ministering 3.

He waited for the Father's timing.

"Mine hour is not yet come."
— *John 2:4 (KJV)*

If Jesus waited, so must you.

WHEN WRESTLING PRODUCES REVELATION

Your struggle with timing is not a waste — it is a womb.

God uses wrestling seasons to birth:

- Revelation
- Refinement
- Renewal
- Resilience
- Realignment
- Recommitment

The wrestle makes you ready.

Jacob wrestled with God until his identity changed.

"…I will not let thee go, except thou bless me."
— *Genesis 32:26 (KJV)*

Wrestling leads to transformation.

THE BEAUTY OF GOD'S PERFECT TIMING

When your moment arrives:

- The door will open effortlessly
- Resources will align quickly
- People will appear suddenly
- Strength will feel supernatural
- Opportunities will confirm themselves
- Peace will settle your spirit
- Favor will surround you
- Acceleration will surprise you

There is nothing like God's timing — it carries ease, clarity, confidence, and peace.

"He hath made everything beautiful in his time."
— *Ecclesiastes 3:11 (KJV)*

Beauty arrives **in** time — not before it.

WHAT TO DO WHILE YOU WAIT

1. Surrender your timeline

Let God hold the clock.

2. Stay faithful

Do what God asked you to do last.

3. Stay expectant

Expectation keeps hope alive.

4. Guard your heart from discouragement

Don't let delay plant seeds of doubt.

5. Speak life over your future

Your words shape your endurance.

6. Prepare for what you prayed for

Preparation is evidence of faith.

7. Worship while waiting

Worship shifts your atmosphere.

8. Watch for God's next instruction

Timing often shifts through guidance.

WHEN GOD'S TIMING ARRIVES — YOU WILL KNOW

There will be no confusion.

No forcing.

No fear.

No chaos.

No uncertainty.

God's timing comes with:
- Confirmation
- Peace
- Flow
- Favor
- Momentum
- Open doors
- Clarity
- Strength

Your spirit will say, **"This is it."**

REFLECTION QUESTIONS — CHAPTER 5

1. What specific promise has caused you to wrestle with God's timing?

2. How do you respond emotionally when delays stretch longer than expected?

3. What fear rises when you think about waiting longer?

4. Which biblical story of divine timing resonates most with you?

5. What area of your life do you feel God is preparing rather than delaying?

6. How can you prepare spiritually for God's timing?

JOURNALING PROMPT — CHAPTER 5

"Lord, help me surrender my timeline, trust your wisdom, and rest in the assurance that your timing is perfect."

Write honestly. Let your heart speak.

CHAPTER 6

WHAT GOD DEVELOPS IN THE DARK

There is a sacred kind of darkness that God uses— not to punish, but to prepare; not to conceal your worth, but to cultivate it; not to hide you from purpose, but to hide purpose *in you*. This darkness is not evil or destructive. It is the quiet, unseen, spiritual womb where God develops His greatest work.

It is uncomfortable.

It is lonely.

It is confusing.

But it is holy.

Your dark season is not the end of you. It is the forming of you.

"He made darkness his secret place…"

— *Psalm 18:11 (KJV)*

God works where you cannot see.

God shapes what you cannot feel.

God builds what you cannot yet comprehend.

DELAYED NOT DENIED

Darkness is God's workshop.

THE DARK SEASON YOU DIDN'T ASK FOR

Every believer encounters a moment they didn't expect:

- The setback that wasn't on your calendar
- The loss that wasn't part of your plan
- The waiting that stretched far longer than you wanted
- The closed door you thought would stay open
- The dream that went silent
- The transition you didn't see coming
- The stillness that replaced momentum
- The disappointment that disrupted hope

This moment leads into a season where everything...

slows down,

quietens,

dims,

stops.

You may feel:

- "God, where are you?"
- "Why is this happening to me?"
- "What am I supposed to learn?"
- "Why does it feel like I'm hidden from everyone—including myself?"

- "Why can't I see progress?"

But hiddenness is one of God's greatest gifts—
though often disguised as abandonment.

Darkness teaches what daylight cannot.

A STORY: WHEN LIFE FORCES YOU INTO HIDING

Angela was a thriving entrepreneur. Contracts were flowing, clients were numerous, and opportunities came from everywhere. Then suddenly—everything slowed.

A major deal collapsed.
A long-term client cut ties.
Her finances dipped.
Her confidence cracked.
Her phone stopped ringing.

She prayed for breakthrough.
She sought advice.
She worked harder.
But nothing changed.

At first she thought she was failing.
Then she thought God was silent.
Then she felt like she was being punished.

But months later—God showed her the truth.

During her dark season:
- Her prayer life deepened
- Her humility increased
- Her financial discipline matured
- Her creativity expanded
- Her priorities shifted
- Her emotional health strengthened
- Her reliance on God—not success—was restored

Then, doors reopened—**better ones**.

God wasn't punishing her.

He was developing her.

The dark season wasn't her downfall.

It was her foundation.

WHAT GOD DOES IN THE DARK THAT HE DOESN'T DO IN THE LIGHT

1. God develops your identity

In darkness, titles disappear. Applause silences. Rewards fade. Expectations dissolve. You discover who you are when all you have is God.

2. God refines your motives

Are you pursuing the promise or the Promiser? Dark seasons reveal intention.

3. God strengthens your endurance

Endurance isn't built in comfort—it's forged in pressure.

4. God purifies your vision

Darkness breaks illusions. You begin to see what truly matters.

5. God eliminates distractions

In obscurity, the unnecessary falls away.

6. God transforms your prayer life

Deep prayer is rarely born in daylight. It grows in shadows.

7. God breaks pride and builds humility

Without hiddenness, elevation would destroy you.

8. God aligns you with His timing

Darkness slows you down so God can speed you up later.

THE DARK ROOM METAPHOR — DEVELOPING WHAT YOU CAN'T SEE

Consider photography.

A powerful image begins as an invisible negative.

It is taken into a dark room.

There, it undergoes chemical transformation.

If the film is exposed too early, the image is ruined.

But if left in darkness long enough, the image becomes clear and strong.

You are God's photograph.

Development requires:
- Time
- Darkness
- Patience
- Stillness

Rushing development destroys clarity.
Remaining in darkness too long isn't the issue—
leaving too early is.

When God hides you, He is revealing what you will become.

"He that dwelleth in the secret place of the most high…"
— *Psalm 91:1 (KJV)*

The secret place is God's dark room.

BIBLICAL SHADOW PLACES WHERE PURPOSE WAS FORMED

Moses — 40 Years in the Shadows
Before he delivered Israel, he disappeared into obscurity.
People forgot him.

Egypt erased him.

His calling seemed abandoned.

But God was shaping:
- Patience
- Humility
- Leadership
- Compassion

Had Moses stayed in Egypt's spotlight, pride would have consumed him.

Joseph — Forgotten in Prison

Sold. Betrayed. Lied on. Buried in obscurity.

But in darkness, God developed:
- Administration
- Interpretation
- Integrity
- Resilience
- Wisdom

Had Joseph reached the palace too early, he wouldn't have the character to handle the position.

David — Trained in the Pasture
While his brothers were seen, David was hidden—
fighting lions, bears, and loneliness.

His greatness was grown in the shadows.

Hannah — Formed Through Pain
Before Samuel was born, her sorrow shaped her prayer life.

Jesus — Silent for 30 Years
The Savior of the world lived hidden, unknown, uncelebrated.

Because God grows greatness slowly.

WHEN THE DARKNESS FEELS LIKE DELAY

Sometimes the hardest part is not the darkness—it's the *waiting.*

You feel like:
- You should be further
- You should be noticed
- You should be promoted
- You should be recognized
- You should be established
- You should be flourishing

But God whispers:

"Not yet."

Because "not yet" means:
- You're growing

- You're becoming
- You're transforming
- You're preparing
- You're maturing
- You're aligning

"To everything there is a season…"

— *Ecclesiastes 3:1 (KJV)*

Your season will come—

but development must come first.

A STORY: THE MAN WHO THOUGHT GOD FORGOT HIM

Marcus felt called to preach at 19.

He studied.

Served.

Read Scripture daily.

Honored leadership.

But for years, no one asked him to speak.

Instead:

- He cleaned bathrooms
- He stacked chairs
- He carried equipment
- He drove the church van

- He mentored youth quietly

He thought God overlooked him.

Then one night, the pastor said:

"Marcus, you're preaching this Sunday."

His message was powerful, mature, and anointed beyond his years.

Later the pastor told him:

"We didn't hold you back.
We held you together until God was ready."

God never forgot Marcus.
He was forming him.

WHAT GOD DESTROYS IN THE DARK

Dark seasons strip away:

- Arrogance
- Entitlement
- Impatience
- Immature ambition
- Emotional instability
- Dependence on people
- Superficial faith

- Weak foundations
- False relationships
- Misaligned desires

God removes what cannot survive your next level.

God subtracts before He multiplies.

WHAT GOD BUILDS IN THE DARK

Dark seasons create:
- Stability
- Consistency
- Spiritual maturity
- Emotional intelligence
- Discernment
- Identity
- Authority
- Vision
- Conviction
- Endurance
- Prayer power
- Wisdom

God invests heavily in the hidden seasons because what comes next requires weight.

Elevation without depth creates collapse.

THE DARKNESS BEFORE THE DAWN

Every dawn has a moment where darkness is deepest.

Right before the sun rises,

right before the light breaks through,

right before the new season begins—

darkness gathers itself.

This is not a sign that things are getting worse.

It is a sign that breakthrough is drawing near.

The darkest moment of your life may be the closest moment to your purpose.

"…weeping may endure for a night, but joy cometh in the morning."

— *Psalm 30:5 (KJV)*

Morning always comes.

THE MOMENT GOD BRINGS YOU OUT OF HIDING

Then suddenly…

- Someone will notice your gift
- A new opportunity will appear

- A divine connection will form
- A door will open that no one can shut
- A season will shift immediately
- A calling will accelerate
- A blessing will manifest fully

And the same people who wondered where you were
will wonder where you *came from*.

You were not missing—
you were in development.

When God brings you into the light, He does so intentionally:

- At the right moment
- In the right environment
- With the right character
- With the right relationships
- With the right mindset
- With the right humility
- With the right endurance

Nothing will be wasted.
Nothing will be out of place.
Nothing will arrive prematurely.

God will reveal you when your development is complete.

REFLECTION QUESTIONS — CHAPTER 6

1. What part of your life feels hidden right now?
2. How have you reacted emotionally to seasons of darkness?
3. What strengths is God developing in you beneath the surface?
4. Which biblical figure's dark season resembles yours?
5. How has God protected you through hiddenness?
6. What might God be preparing you for that requires more growth?
7. What has darkness allowed you to see in yourself?

JOURNALING PROMPT — CHAPTER 6

"Lord, help me embrace my hidden season with faith. Reveal what you are building in me, and give me the patience to grow in the dark until you bring me into the light.

CHAPTER 7

PROTECTED, NOT REJECTED

One of the most painful experiences a believer faces is feeling rejected—by people, by opportunities, by circumstances, or even by timing. Some of life's greatest wounds are formed when something you hoped for slips out of your hands, when someone you trusted walks away, or when a door you believed God would open remains tightly shut.

But here is the truth Heaven wants you to embrace:

Many of the things you interpret as rejection are actually divine protection.

God's "no" is often a shield.
His delays are often detours around danger.
His closed doors are often walls around your future.
His "not yet" is often a "not there."

You think you were rejected.
But God says you were protected.

"As for God, his way is perfect…"
— *Psalm 18:30 (KJV)*

If His way is perfect, then His protection is perfect too.

THE PAIN OF FEELING UNWANTED OR UNCHOSEN

Rejection always hits deep because it attacks identity. It whispers lies:

- "You're not good enough."
- "You're not wanted."
- "You're not valuable."
- "You don't matter."
- "You failed."
- "You're forgotten."

But Heaven speaks a different word:

"Yea, I have loved thee with an everlasting love…"
— *Jeremiah 31:3 (KJV)*

Rejection speaks to your emotions.
Protection speaks to your destiny.

God will let certain people, places, and opportunities turn away from you because they cannot steward what He placed inside you.

Your calling is too big for every crowd.

Your purpose is too valuable for every connection.

Your spirit is too sensitive for every environment.

What you call rejection may actually be **God pulling you out of harm's way**.

A STORY: THE JOB SHE DIDN'T GET

Tanya applied for her dream job. The interview was strong. She felt God's peace about it. She believed the offer was coming.

Then the email arrived:

"We regret to inform you…"

Her chest tightened. Her eyes watered. She felt humiliated. She felt unwanted. She felt confused.

Months later, she learned:

- The department collapsed
- Layoffs swept the entire branch
- The supervisor resigned after conflict
- The company downsized dramatically

She didn't lose an opportunity.

God removed her from chaos.

DELAYED NOT DENIED

What she saw as rejection
Heaven labeled **protection**.

THE REJECTION THAT SAVED YOUR FUTURE

Some relationships didn't work because they would have
damaged you.
Some friendships faded because they would have limited you.
Some jobs fell through because they were beneath your
calling.
Some people walked away because their season in your life
was over.
Some partnerships dissolved because their motives weren't
aligned with God's.

You weren't rejected—
you were rescued.

"No weapon that is formed against thee shall prosper…"
— *Isaiah 54:17 (KJV)*

Sometimes the "weapon" is the wrong person.
The wrong opportunity.
The wrong move.
The wrong environment.

God does not just block weapons—
He blocks access to them.

WHEN GOD PROTECTS YOU FROM WHAT YOU WANTED

Many believers experience the heartbreak of wanting

something deeply…

and God saying **no**.

A ministry you wanted.

A relationship you prayed for.

A position you fought for.

A move you anticipated.

A dream you held tightly.

And God said:

"No.

Not here.

Not them.

Not now."

It feels like rejection, but God sees angles you cannot:

- Motives you can't discern

- Futures you can't predict

- Dangers you can't perceive

- Distractions you can't identify

- Character issues you can't detect
- Spiritual traps you can't sense

God protects you even when you fight for what harms you.

BIBLICAL MOMENTS OF PROTECTION MASKED AS REJECTION

1. Joseph — Rejected by Brothers, Protected by God

Their rejection pushed him toward destiny.

2. David: Overlooked by His Father, Chosen by God

Man's disregard positioned him for divine promotion.

3. Moses: Rejected by Israel, Sent to the Wilderness

The wilderness preserved him until his season.

4. Jesus: Rejected in Nazareth, Received Elsewhere

Rejection redirected Him to those ready to receive.

5. Paul: Forbidden by the Spirit to Preach in Asia

Not a rejection. A redirection.

God uses rejection to reposition.

A STORY: THE RELATIONSHIP THAT ENDED TOO SOON

Darius thought she was "the one."

They had plans. They had chemistry. They had vision. They had connection.

Then one day she ended it. No warning. No explanation. Just gone.

He was shattered.

Months later, he learned:
- She was battling hidden addiction
- Her lifestyle conflicted with his calling
- Her unresolved trauma would have crushed his peace
- Her spiritual instability would have derailed his purpose

What he saw as heartbreak

God saw as safeguarding.

Darius later said:

"God protected my marriage before I even had one."

Sometimes God breaks your heart to prevent a lifetime of brokenness.

GOD'S PROTECTION DOESN'T ALWAYS FEEL GENTLE

Protection can feel like:

- Detours

- Denials

- Delays

- Disappointments

- Disconnections

- Distance

- Discouragement

But with God, pain always has purpose.

"For we walk by faith, not by sight."
— *2 Corinthians 5:7 (KJV)*

You cannot see the danger He is blocking,

but you can trust the hand that shields you.

WHEN GOD REMOVES PEOPLE YOU WANTED TO KEEP

One of the hardest protections is **relational removal**.

People leave.

People change.

People disappoint.

People betray.

People drift.

But here's the truth:

God will never remove someone who is essential to your purpose.

If they left, they were not assigned to your next chapter.

Their part ended.

Their role shifted.

Their season closed.

God has a way of exposing hearts you could not see and revealing intentions you would have ignored.

Rejection?

No —

revelation.

SIGNS THAT YOU ARE BEING PROTECTED, NOT REJECTED

1. The thing you lost begins to make sense later

Clarity always comes in hindsight.

2. Peace returns stronger than before

Protection brings internal calm.

3. You discover something harmful you didn't initially know
God knew it first.

4. Your spirit grows instead of shrinking
Rejection wounds. Protection strengthens.

5. God replaces what you lost with something better
Always.
God's protection is foresight you do not have.

A STORY: THE MOVE THAT DIDN'T HAPPEN

A family tried desperately to move to another city for what seemed like a better opportunity. They prayed, packed, applied, and prepared. But things fell apart.

They stayed.

Two months later:

- A massive storm hit the city they planned to move to
- Their would-be neighborhood was destroyed
- The company offering the job shut down
- The school they planned to enroll in closed
- Crime rates spiked

They cried when the move fell through.
They praised when they realized God protected them.

Sometimes protection looks like inconvenience.

Sometimes protection looks like disappointment.

Sometimes protection looks like failure.

But protection always looks like God's hand.

REJECTION BECAUSE OF ELEVATION

Here is a truth that will shift your perspective:

Some people reject you because they cannot go where God is taking you.

Your growth:
- Intimidates them
- Exposes their stagnation
- Disrupts their comfort
- Challenges their loyalty

They reject you to relieve themselves.

But God removes them to release you.

"And the LORD said unto Abram, after that Lot was separated from him…"
— *Genesis 13:14 (KJV)*

Abram didn't hear God clearly
until Lot left.

Some revelations come only after separation.

THE REJECTION JESUS EXPERIENCED

Jesus Himself was:

- Mocked

- Betrayed

- Abandoned

- Denied

- Misunderstood

- Lied on

- Rejected

But every rejection fulfilled prophecy.

Every rejection pushed Him toward purpose.

If the Son of God experienced rejection but was never rejected by the Father, then you too can endure rejection without losing identity.

TRUTH THAT HEALS THE HEART

Here is what God wants you to know:

You were not rejected. You were redirected.

You were not discarded. You were delivered.

You were not excluded. You were escorted by grace.

You were not pushed aside. You were pulled forward.

You were not forgotten. You were foreknown.

God protects what He values—

and He values *you*.

REFLECTION QUESTIONS — CHAPTER 7

1. What situation in your life felt like rejection but may have been protection?
2. What has God blocked that you wanted—and what might He have seen?
3. How has God used past disappointments to redirect your path?
4. Which biblical example of protection disguised as rejection resonates most?
5. What relationships or opportunities is God asking you to release?

JOURNALING PROMPT — CHAPTER 7

"Father, help me reinterpret my past rejections through the lens of Your protection. Reveal what You were shielding me from, and help me trust You more deeply moving forward."

Write freely. Let God speak.

DELAYED NOT DENIED

CHAPTER 8

THE BEAUTY OF DIVINE REDIRECTION

Redirection is one of the most beautiful, yet often misunderstood, ways God leads His children. We tend to think of direction as a straight line—from where we are to where we believe God wants us to be. But God's guidance rarely moves in a straight line. It twists. It turns. It curves. It pauses. It reroutes.

And at times, it completely changes course.

These moments can feel like setbacks, disappointments, or confusion. You may feel like you've taken the wrong path or missed a crucial turn. But Heaven whispers a truth:

God's redirection is not punishment — it is placement.

It is not God changing His mind — it is God revealing His map.

It is not the end — it is an upgrade.

"A man's heart deviseth his way: but the LORD directeth his steps."

— *Proverbs 16:9 (KJV)*

You make the plans.
God makes the path.

And His path often looks nothing like the one you imagined.

WHEN YOUR PLAN COLLIDES WITH GOD'S PURPOSE

Every believer has had a moment where your personal plans run headfirst into God's intentions. You thought you were going one direction, only to find yourself somewhere completely unexpected.

You planned the route.
God rerouted you.

You expected one outcome.
God orchestrated another.

And although the moment felt like disappointment, later — sometimes years later — you realized:

"God saved me from something I didn't know was ahead. God redirected me toward something far better."

The beauty of divine redirection is that it always leads to purpose, never away from it.

A STORY: THE INTERVIEW THAT DIDN'T HAPPEN

Jordan had prayed for a career shift for years. Finally, an interview came. It was with a company she admired. The opportunity was bigger than anything she'd imagined.

But on the morning of the interview, her car broke down.
She called a rideshare — it canceled.
She tried again — delayed.
She watched the clock tick away.
She realized she wouldn't make it.

She cried.

Not just because she missed the interview — but because she felt she missed her chance.

Three weeks later, the company announced a major scandal.
A senior leader was arrested.
The branch dissolved.
Employees were laid off.

What felt like a tragic inconvenience was actually **divine interruption?**

God's redirection saved her career — and her peace.

DIVINE REDIRECTION OFTEN DISRUPTS YOUR EXPECTATIONS

God will sometimes disrupt:

- Your plans

- Your schedule

- Your assumptions

- Your expectations

- Your timing

- Your desired path

Not to frustrate you, but to prevent you from settling.

Not to confuse you, but to clarify your purpose.

Not to disappoint you, but to deliver you to destiny.

"For my thoughts are not your thoughts, neither are your ways my ways, saith the LORD."

— *Isaiah 55:8 (KJV)*

God is not obligated to follow the route you created.

He follows the route that leads to your purpose.

REDIRECTION IS GOD'S WAY OF SAYING: "I HAVE SOMETHING BETTER."

We often cling to what feels familiar.

We cling to what we think is next.

We cling to what we planned.

But God sees what you cannot see:
- The danger ahead
- The deception in certain connections
- The disappointment behind a temporary opportunity
- The dead end that looks appealing from a distance
- The heartbreak hidden beneath a desire

God's redirection is not a rejection of your dream —

it is a repositioning so the dream can flourish.

BIBLICAL MOMENTS OF DIVINE REDIRECTION

1. Abraham — Redirected from His Homeland

God told Abraham:

"Get thee out... unto a land that I will show thee."
— *Genesis 12:1 (KJV)*

Abraham wasn't given details — only direction.

Redirection birthed a nation.

2. Joseph — Redirected Through Pain

Thrown into a pit.

Sold into slavery.

Imprisoned falsely.

Every painful turn was a redirection toward the palace.

Had Joseph not been redirected, he never would have saved nations.

3. Ruth — Redirected Through Loss

Widowed.

Displaced.

Heartbroken.

But her redirection positioned her directly into the lineage of Christ.

God turns loss into lineage.

4. Paul — Forbidden to Preach in Asia

"…but the Spirit suffered them not."
— *Acts 16:7 (KJV)*

Paul wanted to go one way.
God said no.

Instead, God directed him to Macedonia —
where revival broke out.

God doesn't just redirect — He upgrades.

5. Jesus — Redirected the Disciples Repeatedly

"Launch out into the deep."

"Let us go to the other side."

"Ye shall be witnesses unto all nations."

Redirection was the rhythm of their ministry.

They had plans.

Jesus had purpose.

A STORY: THE SCHOOL HE DIDN'T ENROLL IN

Marcus received acceptance letters from two colleges. He wanted College A — it was prestigious, in a big city, and many of his friends were going there.

College B was quieter, less glamorous, and more isolated.

He chose College A.

But financial aid fell through.

His appeals were denied.

Deadlines passed.

He reluctantly enrolled in College B.

There he met:
- His future wife
- His lifelong mentor

- A professor who opened doors for him
- The ministry that shaped his calling
- The friends who became family
- The opportunity that launched his career

Later he said:

"God redirected my assignment to reveal my destiny."

Had Marcus forced his way into College A, he would've missed everything God ordained.

Divine redirection is God's love disguised as inconvenience.

REDIRECTION SAVES YOU FROM ROOMS NOT BUILT FOR YOU

Sometimes God shuts a route not because it is morally wrong, but because it is **misaligned** with your assignment.

You might have fit into the room,

but the room wouldn't have fit your calling.

Redirection guards:
- Your anointing
- Your mental health
- Your spiritual alignment
- Your emotional wellbeing
- Your purpose
- Your peace

- Your growth

What you think you're losing
God is actually protecting.

WHEN REDIRECTION HURTS

Divine redirection is beautiful —

but rarely painless.

It can feel like:
- Confusion
- Disappointment
- Grief
- Identity crisis
- Frustration
- Isolation
- Fear
- Lack of control

But remember:

Pain is the indicator,

Purpose is the destination.

Redirection isn't God removing you from your story.

It is God rewriting your story.

THE BEAUTY OF ARRIVING WHERE YOU NEVER PLANNED TO BE

Some of the most beautiful moments of your life will be:

- Doors you never expected to open
- People you never expected to meet
- Callings you never expected to carry
- Places you never expected to go
- Roles you never expected to fulfill

All because God redirected you.

Your greatest blessings may not come from the path you planned —

but from the path God rerouted you to.

THE GPS OF HEAVEN

Think of a GPS.

If you take a wrong turn, the GPS recalculates.
If the road is closed, it reroutes.
If traffic is ahead, it adjusts.

You still reach the destination —
just not the way you expected.

God does the same.

DELAYED NOT DENIED

Your delays

Your detours

Your wrong turns

Your disappointments

do not cancel your destiny.

They recalibrate it.

Because:

"The steps of a good man are ordered by the LORD…"
— *Psalm 37:23 (KJV)*

Redirection is God ordering your steps
even when you don't understand the route.

WHEN GOD REDIRECTS THROUGH PEOPLE

Sometimes the people who reject you, oppose you, disappoint you, overlook you, or misunderstand you are unintentionally participating in God's redirection.

They think they are pushing you out.
But they are pushing you *forward*.

They think they are removing you.
But God is relocating you.

They think they are rejecting you.

But God is redirecting you.

People may reroute you,

but they cannot ruin you.

WHEN REDIRECTION BECOMES REVELATION

At some point you look back and realize:

- "God protected me."
- "God preserved me."
- "God upgraded me."
- "God exposed what I didn't see."
- "God saved me from myself."
- "God set me up for something greater."

Redirection is revelation in slow motion.

You understand it only after walking it out.

REFLECTION QUESTIONS — CHAPTER 8

1. What moment in your past felt like rejection but was actually redirection?
2. What path were you committed to that God rerouted?
3. What did God reveal through a detour that you could not see originally?

4. Which biblical example of redirection speaks to you most deeply?

5. What new direction do you sense God leading you toward now?

JOURNALING PROMPT — CHAPTER 8

"Lord, open my eyes to see the beauty in every redirection. Help me release where I thought I was supposed to be, and embrace where You are leading me next."

Write honestly. Let the Spirit guide your pen.

CHAPTER 9

WHEN COMPARISON STEALS YOUR CONFIDENCE

Comparison is one of the most subtle, destructive forces working against your purpose. It creeps into your thoughts quietly and grows aggressively. It steals joy, drains peace, and distorts your understanding of God's timing.

Comparison causes you to question your identity.
Comparison makes you doubt your progress.
Comparison blinds you to your own blessings.
Comparison magnifies others while shrinking yourself.

You begin asking:
- "Why am *I* not further?"
- "Why doesn't my life look like theirs?"
- "Why did they get chosen and not me?"
- "What am I doing wrong?"
- "Is something wrong with me?"
- "Did God forget about me?"

But comparison builds its power on a lie —
that someone else's timeline applies to you.

It doesn't.

"For we dare not make ourselves of the number…
comparing ourselves among ourselves, are not wise."
— *2 Corinthians 10:12 (KJV)*

Comparison is not just unwise —
it is ungodly.
It dishonors the unique call God placed on your life.

You are not behind.
You are not late.
You are not lacking.
You are simply on a different schedule.

THE TRAP OF WATCHING EVERYONE ELSE'S HIGHLIGHTS

We live in a world where everyone's successes are visible:

- Promotions announced
- Engagements celebrated
- New homes posted
- Ministry opportunities displayed
- Business milestones shared
- Books released
- Doors opening everywhere

And while you celebrate others, inwardly you may feel:

- Overlooked
- Delayed
- Forgotten
- Unprepared
- Underdeveloped
- Unseen

You start to think:

"Lord, when will it be **my** turn?"

But God does not bless you according to what others have received.

He blesses you according to *what He prepared for you.*

A STORY: THE FRIEND WHO SEEMED AHEAD

Meagan and Shanice were close friends. Same age. Same career field. Same ambitions.

But Shanice seemed to leap ahead:

- First job
- First promotion
- First home
- First marriage
- First ministry assignment

Meagan was genuinely happy for her friend — and genuinely discouraged for herself.

Late one night, she prayed:

"Lord, I'm grateful, but I feel left behind."

Months later, Shanice confessed privately that the pressure was overwhelming. Her marriage was strained. Her job was draining. Her pace was unsustainable. She envied Meagan's peace, stability, and spiritual growth.

What Meagan thought she lacked
was actually what Shanice desperately needed.

Comparison tells lies about others and hides truths about you.

THE DANGER OF MISREADING SOMEONE ELSE'S STORY

Everyone has:

- Private battles
- Hidden insecurities
- Untold losses
- Unspoken wounds
- Silent prayers
- Unseen struggles

DELAYED NOT DENIED

You may admire a victory they fought hard to earn.

You may covet a blessing they cried through.

You may desire a life they barely survived.

Comparison gives you a filtered view of others but a harsh view of yourself.

GOD'S TIMING DOES NOT FOLLOW HUMAN SCHEDULES

Your journey is handcrafted.

Your calling is customized.

Your preparation is intentional.

Your pace is determined by Heaven.

You cannot rush what God is building.

You cannot imitate what God designed uniquely.

You cannot compare what God personalized.

"My times are in thy hand…"
— *Psalm 31:15 (KJV)*

Your times are not in your friend's hand.

Not in your coworker's hand.

Not in social media's hand.

Not in society's expectations.

Your times are in **God's** hands —
and His timing never fails.

A STORY: THE ENTREPRENEUR WHO "LOST TIME"

Darryl spent years building a business. He watched others scale faster, grow quicker, and succeed louder. He once told God:

"I feel like I'm years behind everyone else."

Then a major shift happened in his industry. Companies around him collapsed because they grew too fast and lacked foundation. But Darryl's "slow" years had given him:

- Stability
- Wisdom
- Financial discipline
- Loyal customers
- Strategic insight

What looked like delay was actually **foundation**.

His slow pace was **protection** disguised as disappointment.

His timing looked off to him.
It looked perfect to God.

COMPARISON BLINDS YOU TO YOUR OWN PROGRESS

You may not see progress because comparison distorts measurement.

You measure:
- Your beginning against someone else's middle
- Your quiet season against someone's highlight reel
- Your preparation against someone else's manifestation
- Your private development against someone's public unveiling

But God measures:
- Obedience
- Faithfulness
- Character
- Integrity
- Growth
- Surrender
- Preparation

He is not watching your speed.

He is watching your readiness.

THE HEAVENLY PERSPECTIVE ON YOUR "SLOW" SEASONS

Slow seasons frustrate the flesh

but develop the spirit.

Slow seasons feel like stagnation

but create strength.

Slow seasons look like delay

but establish depth.

There is beauty in being developed thoroughly.

"They that wait upon the LORD shall renew their

strength…"

— *Isaiah 40:31 (KJV)*

Waiting is not losing.

Waiting is strengthening.

WHAT COMPARISON DOES TO YOUR CONFIDENCE

Comparison can:

- Paralyze creativity
- Silence your voice
- Blur your identity
- Erase your joy
- Magnify insecurities

- Sabotage your decisions
- Create envy
- Birth self-doubt
- Distort your calling
- Shrink your faith

Comparison does not just steal confidence —
it steals clarity.

You stop seeing yourself through God's eyes
and start seeing yourself through someone else's
accomplishments.

HOW GOD BREAKS THE SPIRIT OF COMPARISON

1. He reminds you of your uniqueness
Your assignment is not duplicated anywhere on earth.

2. He reveals the purpose in your pace
Your timing is divinely calculated.

3. He shows you the truth behind others' journeys
Not everything is as perfect as it appears.

4. He refocuses your attention on Him
Eyes on God remove eyes from comparison.

5. He teaches contentment
Contentment is not complacency — it is confidence in God.

6. He reveals your strengths

You have qualities others wish they had.

7. He exposes the danger of where you thought you wanted to be

God protects you from paths not meant for you.

A STORY: THE MINISTRY ASSIGNMENT SHE DIDN'T GET

Latrice was passionate about women's ministry. She applied to lead a team. She prepared. She prayed. She felt qualified.

She wasn't chosen.

Someone else — younger, less experienced, less trained — was selected.

Latrice felt dismissed. She felt unseen. She felt hurt.

But God redirected her to begin a small online Bible study. She thought ten women would join. More than 600 did.

Today her ministry reaches thousands.

What she saw as rejection
God saw as redirection
leading toward expansion.

Had she been chosen by man,
she would have been confined by man.

Comparison told her she wasn't good enough.

God's direction showed she was too called to be contained.

THE FREEDOM THAT COMES FROM ACCEPTING YOUR LANE

Your lane is blessed.

Your lane is anointed.

Your lane is equipped.

Your lane is prepared by God.

You lose momentum when you drift into someone else's lane.

Comparison distracts you.

Purpose re-aligns you.

God is not asking you to be better than someone else.

He is asking you to be faithful to who *He* created you to be.

"…be thou faithful unto death, and I will give thee a crown of life."
— *Revelation 2:10 (KJV)*

Faithfulness brings reward —
not comparison.

REFLECTION QUESTIONS — CHAPTER 9

1. Who or what do you most often compare yourself to?
2. How has comparison distorted your view of your progress?
3. What blessings in your life have you overlooked because of comparison?
4. What has God protected you from by slowing your pace?
5. What strengths do you possess that comparison has blinded you to?

JOURNALING PROMPT — CHAPTER 9

"Lord, deliver my heart from comparison. Help me embrace my own timeline, my own calling, and my own path. Strengthen my confidence in who You created me to be."

Write honestly. Release burdens. Hear God.

CHAPTER 10

WHEN GOD USES DETOURS TO BUILD YOU

L ife rarely moves in the straight lines we imagine. We love clarity, predictability, and control. We love when plans unfold smoothly and steps align neatly. But God does not operate according to human blueprints. He often leads us down roads we never expected, turns we didn't anticipate, and detours we didn't choose.

These detours are not punishments.
They are preparation.
They are construction zones for character, endurance, wisdom, and faith.

God uses detours to build what a direct path never could.

"And thou shalt remember all the way which the LORD thy God led thee…"
— *Deuteronomy 8:2 (KJV)*

"All the way" includes the scenic routes, the confusing turns, the lonely roads, and the unexpected stops.
Every part of your journey is included in God's plan — even the detours.

THE DETOUR THAT DOESN'T MAKE SENSE

Sometimes God's path feels like the long way around.

You thought:

- You would reach that goal sooner
- You would be financially stable by now
- You would be further in ministry
- You would have more opportunities
- You would have started the business
- You would have written the book years ago
- You would have found your purpose sooner

But life took you through:

- Setbacks
- Delays
- Heartbreaks
- Unexpected responsibilities
- Wrong turns
- Burned bridges
- Closed doors
- Seasons of waiting

And you wondered:

"Lord, why am I taking the long way? Why can't I just go straight to where You promised?"

But God sees what the straight path would have cost you.

A STORY: THE PRAYER THAT SHIFTED THE PATH

Elijah wanted to start his own nonprofit. He dreamed big, planned carefully, and prayed for doors to open.

But instead of opportunities, he faced:

- A sudden job loss

- A family emergency

- A relocation he didn't want

- Months of financial strain

Everything seemed backward.

Then God opened a door for him to work under a seasoned community leader in his new city. What Elijah thought was a setback became his training ground.

That leader taught him:

- Fundraising strategy

- Community engagement

- How to deal with conflict

- How to manage staff

- How to run large-scale programs

- How to navigate political structures

Years later, when Elijah launched his own nonprofit, it flourished immediately because of the skills he developed on the detour.

Had God sent him straight to leadership, he would have lacked the experience required.

The detour built what the destination required.

DETROURS ARE CLASSROOMS FOR CALLING

God uses detours to teach lessons that elevate you:

1. Detours build patience

You learn to trust God's timing more than your own.

2. Detours develop strength

Longer roads produce endurance.

3. Detours grow spiritual discernment

You become more sensitive to God's voice.

4. Detours humble you

You learn to rely completely on God.

5. Detours expose hidden weaknesses

God reveals areas needing maturity.

6. Detours foster gratitude

You appreciate blessings more deeply.

7. Detours cultivate wisdom

You learn through experience, not just desire.

THE CHILDREN OF ISRAEL — LED THE LONG WAY ON PURPOSE

When God brought Israel out of Egypt, He didn't take them the shortest route to the Promised Land. Scripture says:

"God led them not through the way of the land of the Philistines, although that was near..."
— *Exodus 13:17 (KJV)*

They were strong enough to walk,
but not strong enough to fight.

If they had taken the straight path,
the battles ahead would have crushed them.

God intentionally redirected them to protect them.

Detours are divine strategy.

Your "wasted time" was actually God saving your future.

A STORY: THE JOB THAT WAS NEVER MEANT TO LAST

Tasha accepted a temporary job after her business failed. She felt embarrassed and frustrated. She felt she was beneath her potential. She told God:

"This wasn't the plan."

But at that job she met:
- Her business mentor
- Her future financial partner
- Someone who connected her to a new opportunity
- A coworker who encouraged her spiritually
- A supervisor who pushed her to dream again

That temporary job prepared her for her comeback.

Years later, she said:

"If God hadn't taken me through that detour, I would've still been walking in circles."

The job wasn't her destination —
it was her transformation.

DETROURS BREAK DEPENDENCE ON SELF

When your plans fall apart, you learn to depend on God in ways you never would have otherwise.

Consider:
- When bills exceeded income
- When opportunities fell through
- When doors closed
- When relationships ended
- When direction felt unclear

You discovered God as:
- Provider
- Protector
- Sustainer
- Comforter
- Counselor
- Guide

The detour introduces you to dimensions of God you would not meet on a straight road.

"Trust in the LORD with all thine heart… and he shall direct thy paths."
— *Proverbs 3:5–6 (KJV)*

God directs —

even when the direction looks inefficient.

DETROURS REVEAL WHO IS WITH YOU AND WHO IS NOT

Some people are only meant for certain parts of your journey.

The detour makes this clear.

It exposes:
- Who is genuine
- Who is seasonal
- Who can handle your calling
- Who is only attached to your blessing
- Who loves you for you
- Who loves you for what you provide

Detours purify relationships.

Those who cannot survive the detour

cannot share the destination.

THE DETOUR OF JESUS — THROUGH SAMARIA

Jesus could have taken a more direct route,

but Scripture says:

"He must needs go through Samaria."

— John 4:4 (KJV)

Why?

Because a woman at a well needed Him.

Because a city needed revival.

Because purpose required a detour.

What looked like a geographic inconvenience
was actually a divine appointment.

Your detours bring you into contact with people, experiences,
and revelations you never would have known otherwise.

Detours are destiny disguised.

THE EMOTIONAL BATTLE OF THE DETOUR

Detours can bring feelings of:

- Confusion
- Discouragement
- Frustration
- Anxiety
- Impatience
- Sadness
- Identity questioning

You feel behind.

You feel delayed.

You feel stuck.

You feel like God is silent.

But the truth is:

You are not behind — God slowed you intentionally.

You are not stuck — you are being shaped.

You are not lost — you are being led.

You are not denied — you are being developed.

A STORY: THE SCHOOL ROUTE THAT CHANGED HIS LIFE

A young man named Terrell used to take the same route home from school. One day, construction forced him to take a detour through a different neighborhood.

That detour led him past a community center.

That community center had a tutoring program.

He stopped in out of curiosity.

A mentor took interest in him.

Terrell discovered a passion for technology.

That passion led him to college.

College led him to a career.

His career elevated his entire family.

One forced detour changed generations.

The road you didn't choose
might lead to the life you're destined for.

DETOURS ARE GOD'S WAY OF BUILDING YOU BEFORE HE BLESSES YOU

Some blessings require:

- Stronger character

- Deeper humility

- Greater wisdom

- Increased maturity

- Heightened discernment

- Refined attitudes

- Stabilized emotions

- Strengthened faith

If God gave you the destination before preparing you on the detour,

the blessing would crush you.

God delays elevation until you are strong enough to carry it.

WHEN YOU FINALLY REACH THE DESTINATION

Eventually, the detour ends.

The road straightens.

The purpose becomes clear.

The promise manifests.

And when it does, you will say:

"If God had taken me the way I wanted,

I would've arrived unprepared."

You will recognize that:
- The people you met on the detour were divine
- The skills you gained were necessary
- The strength you built was essential
- The patience you learned was priceless
- The wisdom you gained was strategic
- The faith you developed was foundational

You were not delayed.

You were developed.

"...all things work together for good..."

— *Romans 8:28 (KJV)*

Even detours.

REFLECTION QUESTIONS — CHAPTER 10

1. What detours in your life have confused or frustrated you?

2. How has God used unexpected paths to build your character?

3. What blessings have come from routes you never wanted to take?

4. How did past detours protect you from something you couldn't see?

5. What is God building in you right now through your current detour?

JOURNALING PROMPT — CHAPTER 10

"Lord, help me trust the roads I didn't choose. Build in me everything the destination will require. Strengthen my faith as You lead me through detours designed for my development."

Write honestly. Allow revelation to come as you reflect.

CHAPTER 11

THE STRENGTH TO ENDURE UNTIL GOD SENDS BREAKTHROUGH

There is a particular type of strength God develops in those He is preparing for breakthrough. It is not the strength that comes from physical ability, emotional toughness, or natural resilience. It is the strength that grows in dark seasons, in waiting seasons, in weary seasons — the strength to endure when nothing is changing, nothing is moving, and nothing makes sense.

Breakthrough requires endurance.

Elevation requires endurance.

Purpose requires endurance.

Destiny requires endurance.

And endurance is not built in moments of victory — but in moments of pressure.

"But he that shall endure unto the end, the same shall be saved."

— *Matthew 24:13 (KJV)*

Some blessings require you to outlast the storm before you can step into the promise.

WHEN YOU'RE TIRED OF BEING STRONG

Very few people will admit this out loud, but many feel it deeply:

"I'm tired of being strong."
Strong for your family.

Strong for your coworkers.

Strong for your ministry.

Strong for your friends.

Strong for everyone who expects you to "bounce back."

Strong for people who don't know you struggle silently.

Strong for situations you didn't create.

Strong even when your own heart feels weak.

But God knows.
He sees the weight you carry.

He sees the pressure you endure.

He sees the tears you hide.

He sees the moments you nearly break.

He sees the prayers you whisper.

He sees the faith you hold onto — even when you feel empty.

And He says:

"My grace is sufficient for thee: for my strength is made perfect in weakness."
— *2 Corinthians 12:9 (KJV)*

God does not ask you to be strong on your own —
He becomes your strength.

THE BREAKING POINT THAT BIRTHS BREAKTHROUGH

Everyone has a breaking point — the moment where:

- Your patience runs out
- Your hope feels thin
- Your emotions collapse
- Your prayers feel repetitive
- Your frustration intensifies
- Your energy drains
- Your faith feels stretched

You think, "I can't do this anymore."

But breakthrough often comes at the edge of breaking.
The breaking point is the birthplace of change.

Not because you force the breakthrough —
but because endurance builds capacity for breakthrough.

"Weeping may endure for a night, but joy cometh in the morning."

— *Psalm 30:5 (KJV)*

Endurance carries you from the night into the morning.

A STORY: THE MOTHER WHO ALMOST GAVE UP

Barbara was a single mother of three. She worked two jobs, attended church faithfully, and prayed for financial relief. Still, the bills stacked, the pressure increased, and exhaustion became her daily companion.

One night she cried out:

"Lord, I'm doing everything I can — where is the breakthrough?"

She wanted to give up.

But the next month:

- A new childcare program reduced her expenses
- A woman at church offered tutoring for her children
- A supervisor created a better shift for her
- An unexpected tax refund came
- A friend helped her fix her car
- Hope returned

Later she realized those resources had been in motion long before she saw them.

Breakthrough was coming

— but her endurance kept her steady until it arrived.

ENDURANCE MAKES YOU SPIRITUALLY UNSTOPPABLE

Endurance is not passive waiting;

it is active trusting.

Endurance says:

- "God, I don't see it yet."
- "God, I don't feel it yet."
- "God, I don't understand it yet."
- "But I still trust You."

The enemy cannot defeat someone who refuses to quit.

Endurance is the evidence that your faith is real.

THE PURPOSE OF ENDURANCE IN GOD'S PROCESS

1. Endurance strengthens your roots

Before elevation, God stabilizes your foundation.

2. Endurance enlarges your capacity
You become capable of handling more.

3. Endurance increases your discernment
You learn what is from God and what is from the enemy.

4. Endurance deepens your gratitude
Breakthrough feels sweeter when you survive the wait.

5. Endurance produces spiritual authority
Your testimony becomes weighty.

6. Endurance silences doubt
When you've been through enough storms,

you stop fearing the rain.

7. Endurance matures your faith
Immature faith desires speed.

Mature faith desires God's will.

A STORY: THE DETOUR THAT BUILT ENDURANCE

Caleb dreamed of preaching internationally. He prayed, prepared sermons, studied Scripture, and served faithfully. But for nearly a decade, no invitations came.

Still, he served.

Still, he studied.

Still, he remained faithful.

What he didn't realize was that God was building:

- Depth
- Humility
- Spiritual authority
- Revelation
- Discipline
- Courage

Then suddenly—doors opened.

Not slowly.

Not gradually.

Suddenly.

He preached in five countries within one year.

His endurance prepared his voice for nations.

THE ENEMY USES DELAY TO DISCOURAGE YOU—GOD USES IT TO DEVELOP YOU

When you feel worn down, the enemy whispers:

- "You'll never make it."
- "You're wasting time."
- "God forgot about you."
- "Nothing is changing."
- "You might as well quit."

But these are lies.

Delay is not denial.

Silence is not abandonment.

Waiting is not wasted time.

Weariness is not weakness.

God is building something in you that will outlast the battle.

"Be not weary in well doing: for in due season we shall reap, if we faint not."
— *Galatians 6:9 (KJV)*

Your breakthrough is attached to your **"if."**

If you faint not.

If you don't quit.

If you keep trusting.

If you keep praying.

If you keep believing.

Endurance unlocks what quitting forfeits.

WHEN YOU FEEL LIKE YOU HAVE NOTHING LEFT

God has a tender way of meeting you at your lowest point.

When Elijah collapsed under a juniper tree and said:

"It is enough; now, O LORD, take away my life…"
— *1 Kings 19:4 (KJV)*

God didn't scold him.

He fed him.

He restored him.

He strengthened him.

He recommissioned him.

Sometimes you don't need rebuke.

You need replenishment.

You need rest.

You need refreshing.

You need reassurance.

God gives strength to the fainting heart.

BREAKTHROUGH REQUIRES SPIRITUAL ENDURANCE — NOT PERFECTION

God never asked you to be perfect.

He asked you to:

- Keep believing
- Keep trusting
- Keep praying
- Keep obeying

- Keep walking
- Keep standing

You can struggle and still endure.

You can cry and still endure.

You can doubt and still endure.

You can feel empty and still endure.

Endurance is not about how you feel —
it's about what you refuse to give up on.

A STORY: THE WOMAN WHO WAITED YEARS FOR HEALING

Michelle battled chronic illness for nearly seven years. She went to countless doctors, prayed fervently, and believed faithfully. Some days she improved. Other days she declined.

She wondered:

"Lord, how long?"

But she kept praying.
She kept praising.
She kept believing.

Years later, after a routine test, her doctor told her:

"I don't know what happened, but everything looks normal."

DELAYED NOT DENIED

Her healing didn't come instantly —
it came through endurance.

Her testimony became a weapon in the mouths of others
facing their own battles.

GOD SENDS STRENGTH BEFORE HE SENDS BREAKTHROUGH

Breakthrough often comes suddenly,
but strength builds gradually.

God strengthens you slowly so He can bless you suddenly.

"They go from strength to strength…"
— *Psalm 84:7 (KJV)*

Every step you take,
every prayer you whisper,
every tear you shed,
every obstacle you overcome —

builds strength.

You may not feel strong.
But you are being strengthened.

You may not see progress.
But you are progressing.

You may not feel victorious.

But you are walking toward victory.

REFLECTION QUESTIONS — CHAPTER 11

1. Where in your life do you feel weary or stretched?

2. What has your current season taught you about endurance?

3. How has God strengthened you in ways you didn't notice until later?

4. What breakthrough are you believing for, and what endurance does it require?

5. How can you remind yourself daily that God is strengthening you?

JOURNALING PROMPT — CHAPTER 11

"Lord, give me strength to endure the seasons where nothing seems to be changing. Help me trust your timing, your purpose, and your promise until breakthrough comes."

Write slowly. Let the Spirit strengthen your heart.

CHAPTER 12

TRUSTING GOD WHEN THE ANSWER IS STILL "NOT YET"

There is a sacred weight to the answer "Not yet." It is not loud like a miracle. It is not clear like a yes. It is not final like a no. It is quiet, stretching, humbling — a whisper that interrupts your desires but protects your destiny.

"Not yet" is God's gentle way of saying:

"Wait with Me.

Walk with Me.

Trust My timing.

Trust My heart.

Trust My wisdom."

It is in these seasons of waiting — long, uncertain, emotionally draining seasons — that your faith is tested, stretched, refined, purified, and strengthened.

You learn more about who God is,

and more about who you are,

in the "not yet" than in the "yes."

THE SILENT STRUGGLE OF AN UNANSWERED PRAYER

There is prayer that is answered quickly.

And there is prayer that Heaven holds carefully.

Some prayers are so connected to destiny

that God refuses to rush the response.

You know you're in a "not yet" season when:

- Nothing you try accelerates the process
- Doors that should open remain closed
- Opportunities stall
- Circumstances freeze
- The same prayer is prayed year after year
- You feel like you're circling the same mountain
- Life keeps saying "almost"
- Heaven keeps whispering "wait"

Waiting becomes a quiet burden you carry:
- in your chest
- in your thoughts
- in your heart
- in your worship
- in your private time with God

DELAYED NOT DENIED

It isn't that you doubt God.

It's that you don't understand the timing.

You ask quietly:

"Lord… why not now?"

THE HOLY TENSION BETWEEN FAITH AND WAITING

Faith says:

"I believe God will do it."

Waiting says:

"I don't know when He will."

And the space between belief and manifestation
can feel like a battlefield.

You fight:
- Discouragement
- Isolation
- Frustration
- Doubt
- Fatigue
- Comparison
- Impatience
- Anxiety

- Impulses to take matters into your own hands

You begin to second-guess the promise itself.

But God has not forgotten.
He has not changed His mind.
He has not abandoned the plan.

"Though it tarry, wait for it; because it will surely come, it will not tarry."
— *Habakkuk 2:3 (KJV)*

The vision may pause,
but it will not fail.

WHEN "NOT YET" FEELS LIKE "NOT EVER"

You may never say it out loud,
but deep in your heart you've wondered:

"Maybe this just won't happen for me."

"Maybe I missed my moment."

"Maybe God is silent because I did something wrong."

But waiting is not punishment.
Waiting is preparation.

Waiting does not mean God is angry.
Waiting means God is intentional.

Waiting does not mean you are behind.
Waiting means your blessing is being aligned.

"The LORD is not slack concerning his promise…"
— *2 Peter 3:9 (KJV)*

His timing is not slow.
It is strategic.

A STORY: THE WOMAN WHO WAITED 14 YEARS

Danielle dreamed of owning a home. She saved, fasted, and declared promises. But every attempt fell through. Banks declined her. Houses sold before she could bid. Something blocked the process every single time.

She questioned God often.

"Lord, am I doing something wrong?"

Then, in her fourteenth year of waiting, God opened the door suddenly. She was approved for a home she didn't even think she qualified for — better location, bigger space, lower interest rate, stronger financial footing.

But the greatest miracle wasn't the house.
It was who she had become while waiting:

141

- More disciplined
- Spiritually grounded
- Financially prepared
- Emotionally stable
- Deeply aware of God's voice

She later realized:
"If God had answered earlier, I would have lost the house — and myself."

"Not yet" was the hand of protection.

"Not yet" was the voice of alignment.

"Not yet" was the wisdom of a Father who knew what she could not.

BIBLICAL WAITING IS NEVER EMPTY

▪ **Abraham waited decades**
Because God builds nations in slow, sacred seasons.

▪ **Joseph waited in prison**
Because character needed shaping before promotion.

▪ **Hannah waited through barrenness**
Because Samuel needed to be born at a prophetic moment.

▪ **David waited after being anointed king**
Because elevation requires emotional and spiritual maturity.

- **Israel waited 400 years**

Because deliverance required Moses.

- **Jesus waited 30 years**

Because His ministry could not begin before the appointed time.

- **The disciples waited 10 days in the upper room**

Because the Holy Ghost comes in fullness, not in haste.

All waiting is purposeful.

Nothing God delays is wasted.

WHY GOD SAYS "NOT YET" — IN DEPTH

1. Because you are not ready yet

Not emotionally.

Not spiritually.

Not mentally.

Not financially.

Not relationally.

The blessing requires a version of you that is still being developed.

2. because the environment is not ready for you

Sometimes God delays because:

- The job is unstable
- The relationship is premature
- The church or ministry is unprepared
- The opportunity needs restructuring
- The person assigned to you is still growing

God aligns environments before He aligns you with them.

3. because premature blessings can harm you
Blessings have weight.

If you receive them too soon, they can crush rather than elevate.

He delays to protect.

4. because your testimony is still being written
The impact of the blessing depends on the depth of the journey.

Your waiting will help set others free.

5. because hurry is the enemy of holiness
God slows you down so He can grow you up.

6. because what's coming is bigger than what you asked for
God won't give you small when He is preparing great.

7. because timing determines influence
Some blessings are meant to appear at specific seasons of life so God receives maximum glory.

WHEN GOD'S TIMING FEELS LIKE SILENCE

Silence is one of the hardest tests.

You pray.

You worship.

You obey.

Yet Heaven seems still.

But silence does not mean absence.

God often works the most when He says the least.

"Be still, and know that I am God..."
— *Psalm 46:10 (KJV)*

Stillness produces knowing.

Waiting produces revelation.

A STORY: THE MAN WHO ALMOST WALKED AWAY FROM HIS CALL

Jerome was called to preach, but for years no one invited him to speak. He studied faithfully but never saw the platform he prayed for.

He almost quit.

But one day, a pastor from another state reached out unexpectedly. He had heard Jerome teach in a small Bible study online. He invited him to preach — and the sermon went viral.

Doors opened everywhere.

Jerome later said:

"If God had elevated me earlier, pride would have destroyed me."

God's "not yet" was mercy.

WHAT TO DO IN YOUR "NOT YET" SEASON

1. Deepen intimacy with God

Don't run from Him — run to Him.

2. Keep your heart soft

Disappointment hardens if you don't guard it.

3. Release the spirit of comparison

Your journey cannot be measured by someone else's blessing.

4. Strengthen your prayer life

Waiting increases spiritual sensitivity.

5. Prepare for the blessing

Write the plan.

Develop the skill.

Build the discipline.

Declutter your life.

Preparation honors God's promise.

6. Watch your words

Your mouth shapes your mindset during waiting.

7. Stay faithful where you are

Faithfulness in the "not yet" sets up the "now."

THE MOMENT GOD SAYS "NOW"

When the wait is over, everything accelerates.

God restores time.

God redeems years.

God restructures circumstances.

God realigns relationships.

God breaks barriers.

God opens doors that should've taken years to open.

When the season shifts,

it shifts suddenly.

"And suddenly there came a sound from heaven…"

— *Acts 2:2 (KJV)*

Suddenly is the reward for faithfully enduring "not yet."

REFLECTION QUESTIONS

1. What area of your life has required the most waiting?
2. How has constant waiting shaped your emotions?
3. In what ways has God protected you through delay?
4. What do you sense God is preparing within you during this season?
5. How can you refocus your trust during long periods of silence?
6. What does your "not yet" reveal about God's love and wisdom?

JOURNALING PROMPT

"Lord, teach me to trust You in the quiet places of waiting. Help me release what I cannot control, believe what I cannot see, and surrender to Your timing with peace. Strengthen my spirit to endure 'not yet' so I may walk boldly into 'now' when You declare it."

CHAPTER 13

WHEN GOD TURNS DELAY INTO DESTINY

There comes a moment in your journey where you finally understand something your heart could not grasp in the earlier chapters of your life:

God was not delaying you.

He was developing you.

He was not denying you.

He was directing you.

He was not punishing you.

He was positioning you.

Every slow season, every unanswered prayer, every closed door, every lonely night, every silent year…
was a seed planted in the soil of destiny.

God's hand has been on you — even when you didn't feel it.

God's purpose has been unfolding — even when you couldn't trace it.

God's timing has been precise — even when it didn't match your own.

Destiny does not arrive in the rush of your desire. Destiny arrives in the rhythm of God's design.

"He hath made every thing beautiful in his time…"
— *Ecclesiastes 3:11 (KJV)*

You are stepping into the "beauty" of what God has been shaping in the unseen places of your life.

THE MOMENT YOU REALIZE DELAY WAS DIVINE

There is a day — it could be a morning, a conversation, a revelation, a breakthrough moment — where everything that felt scattered suddenly lines up. Where everything that confused you suddenly becomes clear. Where everything that hurt you suddenly reveals its purpose.

You will look back and say:
- "If that door had opened, I would have missed what God was preparing."
- "If that relationship had lasted, my purpose would have been compromised."
- "If that opportunity had appeared earlier, I would not have been ready."
- "If that season had ended sooner, I would have lost wisdom I now carry."

- "If God had rushed my story, I would not have become who I am today."

Delay was not wasted time.

Delay was sacred time.

THE DESTINY BEHIND YOUR DISAPPOINTMENTS

Some of the greatest disappointments of your life were actually divine interventions.

God allowed certain things to collapse because He knew:

- They weren't strong enough to carry you
- They weren't aligned with your future
- They would have drained your calling
- They would have damaged your confidence
- They would have distracted you from purpose

You cried over it.

You questioned it.

You grieved it.

You nearly gave up because of it.

But God was protecting the destiny inside you.

"For I know the thoughts that I think toward you... to give you an expected end."
— *Jeremiah 29:11 (KJV)*

Your end is expected by God — not accidental.

A STORY: THE WOMAN WHOSE SETBACK SAVED HER LIFE

Karen worked at a corporate job for over a decade. Out of nowhere, the company announced layoffs — and she was among those let go. She felt devastated. Humiliated. Afraid.

For months she applied for jobs with no success. She felt abandoned by God.

But during that season, she visited the doctor after ignoring symptoms for years. Tests revealed early-stage cancer — caught just in time.

Her layoff made space for a diagnosis that saved her life.

During treatment, she discovered a passion for counseling cancer patients. She returned to school, became licensed, and now leads a program helping women navigate healing.

Had she never been laid off, she would have never discovered her purpose... or her diagnosis.

DELAYED NOT DENIED

What felt like a curse
was actually a covering.

Delay saved her.
Delay led her to destiny.

DESTINY REQUIRES A VERSION OF YOU THAT PAIN PRODUCED

There are parts of your purpose
you could not walk in without having walked through:

- The hurt
- The loss
- The betrayal
- The financial pressure
- The waiting
- The uncertainty
- The disappointment
- The spiritual warfare
- The valleys
- The detours

You didn't grow in the easy places.
You grew in the hard places.

Your tears watered the soil of your destiny.

Your prayers shaped the character of your calling.

Your endurance built the framework of your future.

What the enemy meant for evil,

God turned into ingredients for destiny.

"But as for you, ye thought evil against me; but God meant it unto good…"
— *Genesis 50:20 (KJV)*

The delays that the enemy sent to frustrate you

God used to fortify you.

WHEN YOU REALIZE GOD NEVER STOPPED WORKING

There is a shift that happens in your heart when you see:

- God was answering prayers you forgot you prayed.
- God was preparing opportunities you didn't know existed.
- God was rearranging rooms you hadn't yet entered.
- God was strengthening you for blessings you weren't yet ready for.
- God was fighting battles you didn't know were coming.

- God was aligning relationships that would bless your next season.

God was moving

— slowly, steadily, silently, sovereignly.

Delay was His blueprint.

Destiny was His goal.

THE BEAUTY OF DIVINE SEQUENCING

Destiny unfolds in divine sequence — and God never rushes His sequence.

He aligns:

- The right time
- The right people
- The right opportunities
- The right environment
- The right maturity
- The right emotional state
- The right spiritual capacity
- The right season

Some blessings require other people to be in position first.

Some opportunities require conditions you cannot see yet.

Some promises depend on doors that haven't been built yet.

DELAYED NOT DENIED

When God says "not yet,"
He is adjusting the sequence for your good.

A STORY: THE MAN WHO ARRIVED AT HIS DESTINY LATE — BUT RIGHT ON TIME

Victor loved music. For years he wrote songs no one heard. He auditioned for choirs that didn't choose him. He applied to schools that rejected him.

He assumed he had missed his moment.

But at age 42 — far later than he expected — he joined a workshop for new Christian artists. A producer heard one of his songs and instantly felt the anointing. They partnered together. His music spread across churches, then across states, then across countries.

Victor later said:

"If God had released me in my 20s, the fame would've destroyed me. The spotlight would've crushed me. The pressure would've overwhelmed me."

His delay protected the destiny God ordained.

GOD TURNS DELAY INTO DIVINE REVERSAL

God specializes in turning what looked like setbacks into supernatural setups.

You will see:
- A job loss turn into a business launch
- A heartbreak turn into healing ministry
- A denied loan turn into debt freedom
- A rejected application turn into a better opportunity
- A closed relationship turn into a kingdom marriage
- A season of waiting turn into sudden acceleration

God is the God of reversals.

"And he will restore to you the years…"
— *Joel 2:25 (KJV)*

Not just days.
Not just moments.
Years.

Your delayed years are not lost.
God is restoring them with interest.

WHEN HEAVEN DECLARES "NOW"

After years of development, shaping, pruning, and preparation, destiny enters a moment where God speaks a single word:

"Now."

And what took years to grow
can shift in days.

Doors open quickly.
Favor flows easily.
Connections form effortlessly.
Resources appear supernaturally.
Prayers are answered suddenly.
Purpose unfolds powerfully.

You move from:
Waiting → Walking
Praying → Possessing
Believing → Becoming
Preparing → Performing
Hoping → Harvesting

Acceleration replaces delay.
Fulfillment replaces frustration.
Purpose replaces pain.

DELAYED NOT DENIED

When God says "now,"
the delay ends
and destiny begins.

THE YOU WHO EMERGES AFTER DELAY IS NOT THE YOU WHO ENTERED IT

Delay transformed you.

You enter delay with questions
but exit with clarity.

You enter delay with insecurity
but exit with confidence.

You enter delay with fear
but exit with faith.

You enter delay with weakness
but exit with strength.

You enter delay with confusion
but exit with calling.

You were not buried —
you were planted.

You were not stuck —
you were rooted.

You were not denied —
you were designed.

THE DESTINY AHEAD OF YOU IS GREATER THAN THE DELAY BEHIND YOU

Whatever you lost, God is replacing.
Whatever you endured, God is redeeming.
Whatever you prayed for, God is perfecting.
Whatever you waited for, God is unveiling.
Whatever you survived, God is using.

Your best chapters have not been written.
Your greatest seasons have not yet unfolded.
Your deepest joy is still on the horizon.
Your most impactful purpose is still before you.

God is not done.
Delay was not the ending —
it was the shaping.

Destiny is calling.
Destiny is opening.
Destiny is emerging.
Destiny is unfolding.

REFLECTION QUESTIONS —

1. What delays in your life now appear to have divine purpose behind them?

2. How has God used pain to shape the person you've become?

3. What season are you stepping out of — and what new season do you sense God shifting you into?

4. What have you learned about God's timing that you didn't know before?

5. Where do you feel destiny pulling you in this next chapter of your life?

JOURNALING PROMPT

"Father, thank You for every delay that matured me, protected me, positioned me, and prepared me for what You ordained. Give me courage to walk into my destiny with boldness, faith, and complete trust in Your timing."

CHAPTER 14

Patience That Produces Strength

Patience is not passive. It is not weakness. It is not simply the ability to wait without complaining. Biblical patience is spiritual muscle. It is the strength to remain faithful while everything around you seems to move slower than your hopes, slower than your prayers, and slower than your expectations.

Patience is the power to stand when you feel like collapsing.

It is the courage to believe when you are tired of hoping.

It is the discipline to trust God when answers are delayed.

Most people think patience means doing nothing.

But in the Kingdom of God, patience is doing the hardest thing of all — continuing to believe while nothing appears to be changing.

"But let patience have her perfect work, that ye may be perfect and entire, wanting nothing."

— **James 1:4 (KJV)**

Patience does not just help you wait.

Patience prepares you to **win**.

Why God Builds Strength through Waiting

Every major promise in Scripture was connected to a season of waiting. Not because God was slow — but because the blessing required a stronger vessel.

Abraham had to wait before Isaac arrived.

Joseph had to wait before the palace.

David had to wait before the throne.

Hannah had to wait before Samuel.

Jesus waited thirty years before three years of ministry.

Waiting was not wasted time.

Waiting was training time.

God never releases a heavy blessing into weak hands. He develops the hands first.

"Wait on the LORD: be of good courage, and he shall strengthen thine heart: wait, I say, on the LORD."

— Psalm 27:14 (KJV)

Notice what happens when you wait — **strength comes**.

The Strength You Cannot Learn in Comfort

There are things God will only teach you while you are waiting:

• How to pray when you feel tired
• How to trust when you feel unsure
• How to worship when you feel discouraged
• How to hope when you feel behind
• How to keep going when you feel empty

Comfort builds enjoyment.
Waiting builds endurance.

And endurance is what carries you through destiny.

"Knowing this, that the trying of your faith worketh patience."
— James 1:3 (KJV)

Your patience is being forged in pressure — not pleasure.

A Story: The Athlete Who Almost Quit

There was a young athlete who trained every day for years. He ran harder, practiced longer, and pushed himself beyond his limits. Yet while others were being drafted, recruited, and recognized, his name never came up.

He began to think, *"Maybe I'm not good enough."*

But what he didn't realize was this: while others were being rushed into competition, he was being built for endurance.

Years later, when many of those same athletes were injured, burned out, or broken, he was just getting started.

He didn't just make it.
He lasted.

That is what patience produces — **lasting strength.**

Patience Trains You to Carry What You Asked For

Many prayers are not answered immediately because God knows what the answer will require from you.

You prayed for leadership — but leadership requires patience.

You prayed for influence — but influence requires emotional maturity.

You prayed for growth — but growth requires endurance.

You prayed for breakthrough — but breakthrough requires spiritual strength.

God does not want to give you something that will crush you.

So He builds you first.

"Humble yourselves therefore under the mighty hand of God, that he may exalt you in due time."
— 1 Peter 5:6 (KJV)

"Due time" is not delay.
It is preparation.

What Patience Is Really Producing in You

While you are waiting, God is strengthening:

Your faith — so you don't panic when storms come

Your emotions — so you don't collapse under pressure

Your discipline — so you stay steady when things shift

Your character — so you don't self-destruct in success

Your obedience — so you listen when God speaks

Your endurance — so you finish what God started

The waiting is not empty.

It is full of development.

When Patience Feels Impossible

There will be days when patience feels like a burden. Days when you think:

"I'm tired of waiting."

"I'm tired of being strong."

"I'm tired of holding on."

"I'm tired of believing."

But God sees something you don't.

"My grace is sufficient for thee: for my strength is made perfect in weakness."

— 2 Corinthians 12:9 (KJV)

When you feel weak, God is working at full strength.

Patience Turns Pain Into Power

Every time you choose not to quit…

Every time you choose not to rush…

Every time you choose not to settle…

Every time you choose not to give up…

Your strength increases.

Patience is not passive suffering.

It is active spiritual growth.

The Reward of Patience

The Bible makes this promise:

"He that shall endure unto the end, the same shall be saved."

— **Matthew 24:13 (KJV)**

Those who endure inherit the promise.

Those who wait are the ones who last.

Those who trust God through delay are the ones who step into destiny with power instead of pressure.

Reflection Questions — Chapter 14

1. In what area of your life is God teaching you patience right now?
2. How has waiting strengthened you in ways you didn't expect?
3. What emotions surface when you think about waiting longer?
4. Which Scripture in this chapter spoke to you most?
5. How can you view patience as preparation instead of punishment?

Journaling Prompt — Chapter 14

"Lord, show me what you are building in me through this season of waiting. Help me see patience as strength, not delay."

Write honestly. Let God reveal what He is forming inside you.

CHAPTER 15

Endurance for the Long Journey

Not every victory comes quickly. Some promises take time. Some prayers require perseverance. Some breakthroughs demand endurance that goes far beyond enthusiasm. There is a strength God builds in you that cannot be developed in short seasons—it only comes from walking with Him through long, stretching, testing journeys.

Endurance is the ability to keep going when excitement fades, when answers delay, and when circumstances feel heavy. It is faith that refuses to quit.

"But he that shall endure unto the end, the same shall be saved."
— **Matthew 24:13 (KJV)**

Endurance is not about how fast you start—it's about how faithfully you finish.

Why God Values Endurance

God knows that your future will require stamina. What He has prepared for you will not be light, small, or simple. It will be meaningful. It will be impactful. And it will require a depth of strength that only endurance can provide.

A shallow faith collapses under pressure.
A deep faith stands in storms.

"For ye have need of patience, that, after ye have done the will of God, ye might receive the promise."
— **Hebrews 10:36 (KJV)**

Notice the order:

1. Do the will of God
2. Endure
3. Receive the promise

Many people want the promise without the endurance. But God knows the promise is safest in the hands of those who can last.

A Story: The Woman Who Almost Gave Up

Lena had prayed for healing for years. Some days she felt hopeful. Other days she felt forgotten. Doctors had no answers. Her energy was low. Her patience was worn.

One night she said, *"God, I don't know how much longer I can do this."*

But she kept praying.
She kept believing.
She kept trusting.

And slowly, quietly, God began to restore what had been damaged.

She later said, "The healing didn't just fix my body. It healed my faith."

That's what endurance does—it doesn't just carry you through. It transforms you.

Endurance Is Built in Pressure

You don't develop endurance in easy seasons. You develop it when things feel unfair, slow, confusing, or painful.

"Tribulation worketh patience;
And patience, experience;
And experience, hope."
— **Romans 5:3–4 (KJV)**

God uses pressure to produce patience.
Patience produces experience.
Experience produces hope.

And hope keeps you moving forward when everything else says stop.

The Difference between Stopping and Enduring

Stopping feels like relief—but it costs you your future.
Enduring feels hard—but it protects your destiny.

The enemy doesn't need to destroy you. He only needs to convince you to quit.

But endurance keeps you aligned with God's plan even when it's uncomfortable.

"Let us run with patience the race that is set before us."
— **Hebrews 12:1 (KJV)**

You are not running someone else's race.
You are running the one God set for you.

What Endurance Produces

While you are enduring, God is building:

• Emotional stability
• Spiritual maturity
• Deeper trust
• Stronger prayer life
• Greater discernment
• Unshakeable faith
• Quiet confidence
• Lasting character

These are the things you will need when the promise finally arrives.

Endurance When You Feel Overlooked

Some of the hardest endurance happens when you feel forgotten—when others seem to pass you, succeed before you, or receive what you prayed for.

But God sees every faithful step.

"And God is not unrighteous to forget your work and labour of love."
— **Hebrews 6:10 (KJV)**

You are not invisible to Heaven.

Your Long Journey Has Meaning

Every delay.
Every test.
Every quiet season.
Every unanswered prayer.

It is shaping the person who will carry the blessing.

You are not being stalled.
You are being strengthened.

Reflection Questions — Chapter 15

1. Where in your life do you feel most tired right now?
2. What has God helped you endure in the past?
3. How has endurance deepened your faith?
4. Which Scripture in this chapter encouraged you most?
5. What promise are you holding onto?

Journaling Prompt — Chapter 15

"Lord, give me the strength to endure this season with faith. Help me keep walking even when the journey feels long."

Write what you are trusting God for—and how you will keep going.

CHAPTER 16

Recognizing the Signs of Forward Movement

After long seasons of waiting, silence, and endurance, it can become difficult to recognize when God is actually moving. When you've spent so much time standing still, you may overlook the small but powerful shifts that signal something new is happening. God rarely announces progress with thunder. Most of the time, He whispers it through subtle changes, quiet openings, and gentle realignments.

Forward movement does not always look dramatic. Sometimes it looks like peace. Sometimes it looks like clarity. Sometimes it looks like strength returning to places that were once weak.

"The steps of a good man are ordered by the LORD: and he delighteth in his way."
— **Psalm 37:23 (KJV)**

Even when you feel like you've been standing still, God has been ordering your steps.

Why Progress Often Feels Invisible

When you've been in a season of delay, you become conditioned to disappointment. You learn not to expect much. You guard your heart. You hesitate to hope. And because of that, when God begins to move, it can feel unfamiliar.

Small changes may go unnoticed:
• A new sense of peace
• Renewed motivation
• Open conversations
• Unexpected ideas
• Quiet opportunities
• Improved relationships
• Emotional healing
• Spiritual clarity

These are not random. They are signs.

God always moves internally before He moves externally.

"Behold, I will do a new thing; now it shall spring forth; shall ye not know it?"
— Isaiah 43:19 (KJV)

Sometimes the new thing has already begun—you just haven't recognized it yet.

A Story: The Door That Opened Quietly

Rachel prayed for years for her life to change. She wanted a breakthrough, but nothing seemed to happen. One day she accepted a small volunteer role that felt insignificant. It led to a new relationship. That relationship led to a new opportunity. That opportunity changed her future.

She later said, "It didn't happen all at once. It happened one small yes at a time."

That is how God moves.

Signs God Is Moving You Forward

Here are some of the most common signs that you are entering a new season:

1. You feel internal peace even without answers
God settles your spirit before He shifts your situation.

"And the peace of God, which passeth all understanding, shall keep your hearts and minds…"
— **Philippians 4:7 (KJV)**

2. Old desires no longer satisfy you
God is shifting your appetite for something greater.

3. You are becoming more focused
Distractions fall away when destiny draws near.

4. You are more aware of God's voice
Silence prepares you to hear.

5. Doors begin to crack open
not wide—but just enough for you to step.

6. Your faith grows stronger than your fear
you don't need full clarity to keep moving.

God Moves Before You See Results

You may still be waiting on physical evidence—but spiritual movement is already underway.

"For we walk by faith, not by sight."
— **2 Corinthians 5:7 (KJV)**

Faith recognizes motion before manifestation.

When God Begins to Reposition You

God doesn't just change your surroundings—He changes you.

You begin to:
• Think differently
• Respond differently
• Pray differently
• Hope differently
• Dream differently
• Trust differently

That is forward movement.

Don't Ignore the Small Shifts

Breakthrough is rarely a single moment—it is a series of obedient steps.

"Despise not the day of small things."
— Zechariah 4:10 (KJV)

What feels small today may be the foundation of something big tomorrow.

Reflection Questions — Chapter 16

1. What small changes have you noticed in your life recently?
2. Where do you feel a new sense of peace or clarity?
3. What doors feel like they are beginning to open?
4. Which Scripture encouraged you most in this chapter?
5. How can you stay sensitive to God's movement?

Journaling Prompt — Chapter 16

"Lord, open my eyes to the signs of Your movement in my life. Help me recognize when You are leading me forward."

Write what you sense God shifting in you.

CHAPTER 17

When the Promise Feels Distant

There are moments in every believer's life when the promise God gave feels far away. You remember what He spoke. You remember the hope it stirred in your heart. You remember the fire you once carried. But now, time has passed, and nothing seems to have changed. The distance between where you are and where you thought you would be feels wide and heavy.

When the promise feels distant, doubt tries to creep in. You may start wondering if you misunderstood God, if you missed your opportunity, or if the promise was ever meant for you at all. But distance does not mean disconnection. God is still working, even when the promise feels far away.

"Faith is the substance of things hoped for, the evidence of things not seen."
— Hebrews 11:1 (KJV)

Faith believes even when the evidence is not yet visible.

Why Promises Often Feel Far Away

God does not reveal the full timeline of His plans. He gives promises to anchor your faith, not to satisfy your curiosity. When time stretches, it is not because God forgot—it is because God is preparing you for what the promise will require.

You may feel far from what God showed you, but you are closer than you think.

"The LORD is not slack concerning his promise... but is longsuffering..."
— 2 Peter 3:9 (KJV)

Delay is not neglect. It is divine patience.

A Story: The Man Who Almost Let Go

Andre knew God had called him to do more. He felt it in his spirit. But years passed, and nothing changed. He stayed in the same job. The same routine. The same struggle.

One day he said, "Maybe I imagined it."

But shortly after, God began shifting things quietly—new relationships, new ideas, new opportunities. What Andre thought was distance was actually God aligning the path.

The promise didn't disappear. It was getting closer.

Distance Does Not Cancel Destiny

The enemy wants you to believe that time cancels calling—but God says otherwise.

"The gifts and calling of God are without repentance."
— Romans 11:29 (KJV)

What God spoke over you still stands. Even if it feels far away, it is still alive.

How to Hold On When the Promise Feels Far

1. Remember what God said
Write it down. Speak it aloud. Let it anchor you.

2. Refuse comparison
someone else's timing is not your timeline.

3. Stay connected to God

Your relationship with Him keeps the promise alive.

4. Don't let discouragement decide your future

Feelings change. God's Word does not.

5. Keep taking faithful steps

Movement, even small, keeps hope alive.

God Is Working in the Distance

Just because you cannot see the answer doesn't mean it is not being prepared.

"For the vision is yet for an appointed time… though it tarry, wait for it."
— **Habakkuk 2:3 (KJV)**

The promise has a time. And it is on schedule.

Reflection Questions — Chapter 17

1. What promise feels distant right now?
2. How have you been tempted to doubt God's timing?
3. What Scriptures help you stay hopeful?

4. What steps can you take to keep believing?

5. How can you strengthen your trust while you wait?

Journaling Prompt — Chapter 17

"Lord, help me trust You even when Your promise feels far away. Renew my hope and remind me that You are still working."

- Write about the promise you are waiting for and how you will keep believing.

CHAPTER 18

The Breakthrough behind the Delay

There comes a moment in every believer's journey when clarity replaces confusion and understanding replaces frustration. It is the moment you realize that what felt like a delay was actually a doorway to something greater. The waiting, the silence, the setbacks, and the closed doors were not barriers to your breakthrough—they were the very path leading to it.

God does not waste seasons. He does not pause purpose without reason. What you experience as delay is often God working behind the scenes, aligning circumstances, preparing hearts, and shaping you for what is next.

"And we know that all things work together for good to them that love God, to them who are the called according to his purpose."
— **Romans 8:28 (KJV)**

The breakthrough is not just ahead of the delay—it is hidden within it.

Why Breakthrough Often Comes After Delay

God delays not because He is withholding, but because He is preparing. Some breakthroughs require alignment that only time can produce. Others require growth that only pressure can develop.

Delay builds:
- Capacity
- Discernment
- Character
- Humility
- Wisdom
- Dependence on God

Breakthrough without preparation would collapse you. God ensures that when the door opens, you are strong enough to walk through it.

"Humble yourselves therefore under the mighty hand of God, that he may exalt you in due time."
— 1 Peter 5:6 (KJV)

"Due time" is when preparation meets opportunity.

A Story: The Opportunity That Came at the Right Time

Caleb prayed for advancement for years. When opportunities came early, they didn't work out. He felt overlooked and frustrated. But during the waiting years, he gained experience, wisdom, and confidence.

When the opportunity finally came, it came quickly—and he was ready. The delay had sharpened him.

He later said, "If it had happened earlier, I would have failed."

That is the breakthrough behind the delay.

God's Timing Reveals God's Wisdom

What feels late to you is often perfectly timed by God.

"He hath made everything beautiful in his time."
— **Ecclesiastes 3:11 (KJV)**

Breakthroughs arrive when:
• The environment is ready
• The people are aligned

- The foundation is secure
- Your heart is prepared

God sees the full picture.

When Delay Protects You

Some delays save you from:
- Premature success
- Wrong relationships
- Misaligned opportunities
- Spiritual burnout
- Emotional overload

You may have prayed for speed, but God chose safety.

"The LORD shall preserve thee from all evil."
— **Psalm 121:7 (KJV)**

Protection is part of breakthrough.

Breakthrough Is More Than a Moment

Breakthrough is not always instant. Sometimes it unfolds over time. Sometimes it begins internally before it appears externally.

When breakthrough starts, you may notice:
• Renewed energy
• Clear direction
• Open conversations
• Confirmed decisions
• Unexpected favor
• Peace in movement

These are signs that the delay has served its purpose.

Trusting God When You Can't Trace Him

You won't always understand the delay until after the breakthrough.

"For we walk by faith, not by sight."
— 2 Corinthians 5:7 (KJV)

Faith trusts God's process even when it feels slow.

The Testimony That Comes From Delay

One day, you will tell the story of how God brought you through. The delay will become your testimony.

You will say:
- "Now I understand."
- "Now I see."
- "Now I'm grateful."
- "Now I'm ready."

God will use your waiting to encourage others.

Reflection Questions — Chapter 18

1. What delay in your life might be preparing you for breakthrough?
2. How has waiting strengthened you?
3. What would have happened if the breakthrough came earlier?
4. Which Scripture spoke to you most in this chapter?
5. How can you trust God more fully during delay?

Journaling Prompt — Chapter 18

"Lord, help me trust that my delay is part of your divine design. Show me the breakthrough you are preparing behind the scenes."

Write about what you are waiting for—and how you will trust God.

_____

_____

_____

_____

_____

_____

_____

_____

_____

_____

CHAPTER 19

Walking Boldly Into Your Next Season

There comes a sacred moment when waiting ends and movement begins. It is the moment God invites you to step forward—not timidly, not cautiously, but boldly—into the season He has been preparing you for all along. After delays, development, and divine redirection, this is the season where you begin to walk in what God promised.

Boldness is not arrogance.
Boldness is confidence rooted in God's faithfulness.

You are not stepping forward alone—you are stepping forward with everything God has built inside you during the waiting.

"Be strong and of a good courage… for the LORD thy God is with thee whithersoever thou goest."
— **Joshua 1:9 (KJV)**

This is not the time to shrink back. This is the time to rise.

Why Your Next Season Requires Courage

New seasons always feel unfamiliar. Even when you prayed for change, walking into it can feel uncomfortable.

Growth stretches you. New assignments test you. New blessings demand new levels of faith.

But fear is not a sign that you're in the wrong place. It's often a sign that you're stepping into something meaningful.

"God hath not given us the spirit of fear; but of power, and of love, and of a sound mind."
— **2 Timothy 1:7 (KJV)**

Fear tries to keep you stuck in old seasons.
Faith pulls you into new ones.

A Story: The Door He Almost Didn't Walk Through

Marcus waited years for his opportunity. When it finally came, he hesitated. The door was open—but doubt whispered, *"What if you fail?"*

He stepped anyway.

That decision changed everything.

Many people miss their next season not because the door didn't open—but because fear stopped them from walking through it.

What God Has Prepared in You

You are not the same person you were when the delay began. You are wiser. Stronger. More grounded. More spiritually aware. More emotionally stable.

God used the waiting to:
• Heal you
• Strengthen you
• Clarify your calling
• Remove distractions
• Build endurance
• Deepen your faith

You are ready.

"For the LORD shall be thy confidence."
— **Proverbs 3:26 (KJV)**

Walking Forward Without All the Answers

God does not require you to know everything—He only asks you to trust Him.

"Trust in the LORD with all thine heart… and he shall direct thy paths."
— **Proverbs 3:5–6 (KJV)**

Your next step does not require perfect clarity—just obedience.

Letting Go of the Old Season

You cannot carry yesterday into tomorrow. Some things must be released so you can receive what's next.

Let go of:

• Past disappointments

• Old wounds

• Missed expectations

• Fear-based thinking

• Self-doubt

God is calling you forward—not backward.

Your Next Season Is Already Blessed

God has gone ahead of you.

"The LORD shall go before thee."
— **Deuteronomy 31:8 (KJV)**

You are not walking into uncertainty—you are walking into alignment.

Reflection Questions — Chapter 19

1. What new season do you feel God leading you into?
2. What fears try to hold you back?
3. How has God prepared you through the waiting?
4. Which Scripture encouraged you most?
5. What step of faith can you take this week?

Journaling Prompt — Chapter 19

"Lord, give me courage to walk boldly into the season you have prepared for me. Help me trust you with every step."

Write what God is calling you to step into

CHAPTER 20

You Were Never Denied—Only Prepared

There comes a moment in every journey when everything finally comes into focus. The waiting, the silence, the closed doors, the disappointments, the long nights of wondering—all begin to make sense. You realize that what once felt like denial was actually divine preparation.

God never stopped working.
He never stopped planning.
He never stopped protecting.
He never stopped shaping you.

You were never forgotten.
You were being formed.

"He hath made everything beautiful in his time."
— **Ecclesiastes 3:11 (KJV)**

God's timing was not late.
It was perfect.

Looking Back With New Eyes

When you look back now, you can see it clearly:

The doors that closed saved you.
The delays strengthened you.
The detours protected you.
The quiet seasons deepened you.
The struggles refined you.

What felt like rejection was really redirection?
What felt like punishment was really preparation?

"For I know the thoughts that I think toward you, saith the LORD... to give you an expected end."
— **Jeremiah 29:11 (KJV)**

God never changed His mind about you.

A Story: The Dream That Arrived Late

Naomi dreamed of owning her own business. Years passed. Setbacks came. Opportunities slipped away. She thought she missed her moment.

But when her dream finally arrived, she had more wisdom, more stability, and more confidence than ever before.

She later said, "If it had happened earlier, I wouldn't have been ready."

God's preparation made the dream sustainable.

What God Was Doing While You Waited

While you were waiting, God was:
• Strengthening your faith
• Healing your heart
• Teaching you patience
• Removing what didn't belong
• Preparing the right connections
• Aligning circumstances
• Building your character

Nothing was wasted.

"The steps of a good man are ordered by the LORD."
— Psalm 37:23 (KJV)

Every step—even the slow ones—was part of His plan.

Your Delay Was Divine

Delay is not denial—it is development.

God used time to shape you into someone who could carry what He promised.

"Wait on the LORD... he shall strengthen thine heart."
— **Psalm 27:14 (KJV)**

You are stronger now than when you first prayed.

Walking Into What God Prepared

Now you step forward with clarity, confidence, and courage. You understand that the journey mattered just as much as the destination.

God didn't withhold from you—He invested in you.

Your story is not over.
Your purpose is not lost.
Your promise is not cancelled.

Reflection Questions — Chapter 20

1. How has God used delay to prepare you?
2. What are you grateful God did not give you earlier?
3. How has your faith grown through waiting?
4. Which Scripture encouraged you most in this book?
5. What do you feel God is calling you into now?

Journaling Prompt — Chapter 20

"Lord, thank You for every season of preparation. Help me walk forward in confidence, knowing I was never denied— only prepared."

Write a closing prayer or declaration of faith.

_____

_____

_____

_____

_____

_____

_____

FINAL PRAYER

Father, in the name of Jesus, I come before You with a heart full of gratitude. Thank You for every chapter of my life — the ones that made sense immediately and the ones that only made sense in hindsight. Thank You for the delays that protected me, the detours that redirected me, the disappointments that developed me, and the waiting seasons that deepened me.

Lord, I surrender my timeline and embrace Your timing. I yield my desires, my assumptions, my expectations, and my fears to Your perfect will. You are the God who sees the end from the beginning, and You know exactly what I need, when I need it, and how it must unfold. Help me to trust Your process as deeply as I trust Your promise.

Strengthen my heart when patience feels heavy. Renew my faith when doubt tries to whisper. Remind me of Your Word when my emotions feel overwhelmed. Lift my spirit when discouragement knocks at my door. And steady my feet when the path seems unclear.

Lord, teach me to rest in the truth that delay is not denial. Your Word declares, "The vision is yet for an appointed time… though it tarry, wait for it" (Habakkuk 2:3 KJV). Help

me to wait with expectation, hope, and confidence —
knowing that what You have spoken, You will bring to pass.

Father, I thank You for the destiny that awaits me. I thank
You for the doors You are preparing, the opportunities You
are aligning, the relationships You are orchestrating, and the
blessings You are releasing in Your perfect season. I thank
You for the strength I've gained, the wisdom I've earned, the
battles I've survived, and the faith that has grown through
every delay.

Now, Lord, position me for the "suddenly" You have
ordained. Prepare my hands for what I will carry. Prepare my
heart for what I will walk into. Prepare my mind for what I
will become. And prepare my life for every promise that is on
the way.

Father, let my story be a testimony of Your faithfulness. Let
my journey bring others hope. Let my waiting produce fruit.
Let my life shine as evidence that You are not a God of
denial, but a God of perfect timing.

I declare by faith that what You have prepared for me will
manifest. What You've spoken over my life will not fail. What
You've promised will come to pass. My delays are turning
into destiny, my waiting is turning into breakthrough, and my
faith is turning into fulfillment.

Thank You, Lord, for walking with me through every season
— the quiet, the painful, the confusing, the stretching, and
the victorious. I give You glory for the story You are writing.
And I praise You in advance for the good that is still to come.

In Jesus' name,
Amen.

REFLECTION

What God has done-and is still doing- through delay, development, and destiny.

_____

_____

_____

_____

_____

_____

_____

_____

_____

_____

_____

Reflection Page 1 — What Delay Taught Me About God

- What have I learned about God's character during my waiting season

_____

_____

_____

_____

- How has my understanding of His timing changed?

_____

_____

_____

_____

Reflection Page 2 — What Delay Revealed About Me

- What weaknesses, fears, insecurities, or hidden strengths surfaced during my season of delay?

_____

_____

_____

_____

_____

_____

_____

Reflection Page 3 — The Most Painful "Not Yet" I Survived

- What was the hardest moment of waiting I endured, and how did God meet me in that moment?

_____

_____

_____

_____

_____

_____

Reflection Page 4 — Doors God Closed to Protect Me

- Which opportunities, relationships, or desires didn't work out — and what dangers might God have shielded me from?

_____

_____

_____

_____

_____

_____

Reflection Page 5 — The Detours That Developed Me

- What unexpected path or turn in my life shaped me the most?

_____

_____

_____

_____

- How am I different because of it?

_____

_____

_____

_____

Reflection Page 6 — What God Built in the Dark

- What strength, character, wisdom, or faith did God cultivate in me during seasons of hiddenness or silence?

_____

_____

_____

_____

_____

_____

Reflection Page 7 — Moments When Comparison Tried to Steal My Confidence

- Where did comparison affect my journey, and what truth can I hold onto to stay focused on my own path?

_____

_____

_____

_____

_____

_____

_____

Reflection Page 8 — Lessons I Learned While Waiting

- What practices or revelations kept me grounded during long seasons of "not yet"?

_____

_____

_____

_____

_____

_____

_____

_____

Reflection Page 9 — How God Repositioned My Life

- Where can I now see God's redirection at work — even when I didn't understand it at the time?

Reflection Page 10 — The Strength I Discovered in Myself

What strengths or abilities emerged from situations where I felt overwhelmed or exhausted?

_____

_____

_____

_____

_____

_____

_____

Reflection Page 11 — The Destiny God Is Preparing Me For

- Based on everything I've walked through, what future assignment, calling, blessing, or opportunity do I sense God aligning me for?

Reflection Page 12 — My Declaration of Faith Moving Forward

- Write a personal declaration that affirms your trust in God's timing, your faith in His promises, and your belief that *delay is not denial.*

S

ABOUT THE AUTHOR

Ethan L. Ketterer is a dynamic faith-based author, speaker, and visionary leader whose mission is to help individuals recognize that every delay, detour, and moment of waiting can become a launching point for purpose. As the creator of the KTURN brand—*Making a Turn for the Better*—Ethan develops life-changing books, journals, and motivational resources that empower readers to grow spiritually, emotionally, and personally.

Ethan is the author of several impactful works, including *A Seat at the Table*, *The Power of Her Presence*, and other transformational titles under the KTURN banner. His writing blends biblical truth, compassionate insight, and real-world wisdom to guide readers through seasons of transition, healing, leadership, and spiritual development.

Rooted in authenticity and shaped by his own experiences of endurance and transformation, Ethan's voice encourages people to trust God wholeheartedly—even in seasons when answers seem slow, doors remain closed, or life shifts unexpectedly. His passion is to help others understand that delays are often divine setups, preparing them for greater purpose, deeper growth, and stronger faith.

Through the KTURN brand, Ethan continues to inspire individuals, families, educators, and communities to embrace change, pursue purpose, and make intentional turns toward a brighter, stronger, more empowered future.

Whether writing, teaching, creating tools for personal development, or advancing the KTURN movement, Ethan remains committed to one central message:

God has not denied you—He is preparing you for destiny.

DELAYED NOT DENIED

DELAYED NOT DENIED